BERNICE RUBENS

When I Grow Up

LITTLE, BROWN

LITTLE, BROWN

First published in Great Britain in November 2005 by Little, Brown

Copyright © Bernice Rubens 2005
Introduction © Beryl Bainbridge 2005

A CIP catalogue record for this book
is available from the British Library.

ISBN 0 316 73127 7

Typeset in Ehrhardt by M Rules
Printed and bound in Great Britain
by Mackays of Chatham plc, Chatham, Kent

Little, Brown
An imprint of
Time Warner Book Group UK
Brettenham House
Lancaster Place
London WC2E 7EN

www.twbg.co.uk

When I Grow Up

INTRODUCTION

In the last paragraph of this, Bernice Rubens' last book, she writes of her intention to construct a novel that would be a story about the writing of a memoir. In the avoidance of hurt to persons still living it would contain numerous omissions; people, after all, are more important than literature. All the same, it would be a novel about truth, narrated not in the first person but the third person, for 'in that thorny pronoun there is only the past. "I" is final. "I" is the recognition of death.' Some eight months later she died. She had written twenty-five novels, one of which, *The Elected Member*, won the 1970 Booker Prize.

We talked on the telephone about the difficulties of writing a memoir, this one, that is. I held it as a curious fact that, as one grows older, although we have difficulty in remembering what happened the day before yesterday, we can recall in detail the events of fifty years before. This, I believe, is common to all; adult life accelerates, childhood dawdles. And I told her that I didn't think we ever knew the truth, that the truth was always a one-sided judgement, a lie that hadn't been found out, and that as time passed things appear in a different light. 'They don't for me,' she said. 'Not for me.'

We first met in 1977 when taking part in a writers' group travelling around Israel. It wasn't an immediate friendship, and indeed if Bernice had been a different person might never have developed at all, for I insisted on visiting Yad Vashem, the museum of the Holocaust, and crassly asked her to come with me. She refused, and when I returned, visibly shaken, took me aside and explained her reasons. It was comparatively easy, she said, for a non-Jew to feel emotion at such a memorial to man's inhumanity to man, but for a Jew tears are not enough, can never wash away the pain.

Over the next five years we met at various literary festivals. Then I discovered that I had known her brother Cyril years ago in Liverpool when he was playing in the first violins of the Philharmonic Orchestra. My then husband, the painter Austin Davies, had painted his portrait. After this revelation we met at least once a fortnight for the next thirty-odd years, and spoke on the phone in-between.

Some of our closeness was due to a certain similarity in the way our lives had begun, and progressed. As children we had both felt out of step, told lies, felt we were hard done by. As adults we had loved the men we married and they had walked away, crashing our hopes, after which we had gone in for gentleman callers. Both of us used fiction to make sense of the past. Both of us believed that had we been happier neither of us would have needed to write. The title of her memoir, *When I Grow Up*, is apt;

we were both waiting for that to happen.

In other ways we were opposites, which was obviously due to background, myself coming from Liverpool and she a product of a persecuted race seeking a new life in America, where her dad had set sail for in the years before she was born, alighting at Cardiff mistaking it for Chicago. When praised I took refuge in a smirk; Bernice lashed out. When confronted with tragedy I shed tears and crept away; she made enquiries and organised relief. The one thing in which we were equal was our devotion to cigarettes. We smoked as if there was no tomorrow, which of course there isn't.

We rarely talked about actual writing, though at odd moments, mostly in her car, Bernice would mention fleetingly that she'd had a new idea for a book. She never elaborated, which was just as well for her driving was erratic and I referred to her as the Miss Magoo of the open road. Once, driving the wrong way down a street in Mayfair, she spotted the urgent scurrying of four men carrying something slung inside a tablecloth. Reversing to a blast of horns from the traffic behind, she pushed me out of the car. 'Tell them,' she ordered, 'that I'll take them to hospital.' When I caught up with the cortège the injured party turned out to be a large dog who, according to its owner, was out for the count after lapping up the contents of a spilled bottle of wine.

Bernice wrote every day, working in pencil, and never knew from one page to another where the story was leading. Even so, her plotting was immaculate. I went to the launches of her books and she to mine, but we never discussed their contents. Mostly we talked about our beloved grandsons, Josh and Dash, Charlie and Bertie, who are all of a similar age. When we weren't boasting about them – their looks, their scholastic achievements, their obvious inheritance of our own singular talents – we argued about the soaps, in particular *Coronation Street*. We almost fell out over who was to blame when Deirdre went off with that foreigner who was too young for her. Bernice said age had nothing to do with it, that it was the brain that governed attachments. I thought that was rubbish, seeing as neither of us had ever fallen for anyone for reasons higher than the waist. Had we done so, maybe we wouldn't have ended up alone.

To be with Bernice was always exhilarating, if sometimes nerve-racking, for in social circles I was a coward and she was a warrior. If some poor soul embarked on an appraisal of South Africa, or mentioned that so-and-so was very nice even if his name was Finkelstein, she would waste no time in sorting them out. I usually ran off before things got hectic. Her circle of friends was large, and she entertained regularly in each of the successive flats she occupied in the region of Belsize Park. When her oven got too messy or the books overflowed her shelves she sold up, packed up and moved down the road. She was generous, immensely so. When her book *Mother Russia* made a lot of money she invited Paul Bailey, Jeremy Trevathan and myself, along with Cyril and Janet, to stay in a villa in Majorca. We sunbathed all day and played charades into the moonlit small hours.

I knew Bernice's family; lovely Harold, Janet, Cyril and Beryl, lovely daughters, Sharon and Rebecca. I went to family birthdays, weddings and funerals; I even knew her Mom, who I met on Christmas Eve when she was staying with Bernice. For some unexplained reason my taxi driver came upstairs and lay on the bed beside her until almost midnight.

The last time I saw Bernice, before she became ill that is, was at the home of our close friends Mike and Parvin Laurence, on the Isle of Wight. She was not quite herself, more introspective than usual. I remember she sat on a wall gazing out at the sea and remarked that it made her feel calm to look at the water. The very last time I saw her was in hospital, unable to speak. Only her eyes looked at me; I still see them . . . looking.

This isn't an appraisal of a brilliant novelist, simply my own brief memoir of a beloved friend.

Beryl Bainbridge
August 2005

Jacqui Koven, Bernice, Nan and Beryl B., Majorca, 1991

PART ONE

We lived at number nine Glossop Terrace. I was probably born in that house but I never liked to ask. Ours was the last house and one of the terrace's only two private dwellings. The other was number one, at the beginning, and was occupied by a Mr and Mrs Comely. The Comelys and the Rubens acted as book ends to numbers two to eight in between. These seven houses constituted the maternity block of the Cardiff General Hospital. My mother was proud of her neighbours and when my sister Beryl once had the courage to ask where babies come from, my mother told her without hesitation, 'From Glossop Terrace, of course,' as if our address were the fount of creation. It was as though she had to offer some compensation for the fact that we lived in the district of Splott, the unmentionable and indisputable armpit of Cardiff.

The Comelys were a childless couple and there came a

time when they moved from the terrace, possibly sensing their barrenness as a blot on the fecund landscape. The maternity block stretched one house more and we were left as the only private dwelling on the terrace. We could afford to stay after all, and without shame. By then there were four of us children, so we had done our bit by prop-agation.

I was glad when the Comelys left, and mightily relieved. I had had a bizarre encounter with Mrs Comely a week before they moved. I was about six years old and was on my way home from Tredegarville Infant School, at the end of the terrace.

'How's your Mummy and Daddy?' she asked.

'They've gone to South Africa,' I said.

I don't know why I said it. My Mom and Pop didn't have the fare to get to London, leave alone Johannesburg. I ran home with the intention of keeping my parents indoors. But given the six-week boat trip to Cape Town, there and back, and the two weeks at least that they would have to stay there, I was sentencing my parents to an eight-week stretch. Impossible. My mother would tell Mrs Comely that I had a vivid imagination and she would come home and give me what for. So I rejoiced when I saw the removal van jerk out of the terrace. I no longer had to care where or when my parents went, or for how long. But I wondered about that Comely tale I had come up with, where it had surfaced from and why. Mom's ver-dict of overimagination was generous. As a child I was simply a liar by nature, and that Comely story was a whopper. Though I didn't realise it at the time, I was happily at home with mendacity. It was less boring than the truth. My natural home lay in fiction. But it would be some years before I seriously settled into those quarters.

Although we didn't all live together, we were, in essence, an extended family. My grandparents, aunts and uncles lived in Riverside, a twenty-minute tram ride from the fount of creation. The district of Riverside was only marginally upmarket to Splott. It was a Jewish area since it lay within walking distance of the main synagogue in Cathedral Road. There was another synagogue in Cardiff. There had to be a second one so that they could quarrel with each other. Both were orthodox – in those days there was none of that new-fangled reform or liberal fashion. Convenience religion had not yet crossed the Welsh border, and in Cardiff you went to pray on foot. Men were separated from the women and the Service, whether you understood it or not, was in Hebrew entire.

Every Friday evening, despite the embargo on Sabbath travel, the Rubens took the tram ride over the river, to celebrate the onset of the Sabbath at my grandmother's house. Although we kept a strictly kosher household and observed all the festivals, we sometimes broke the rules. We had to. My father worked on Saturdays. It was his busiest day of the week. My Grandma, Millie, preferred to be ignorant of our transgression, and as soon as we arrived on a Friday she urged us to rest since the long walk from Splott must have been tiring. We all feigned fatigue, resting ourselves while she made the final preparations for our Sabbath supper.

The house was crowded. Aunts, uncles, cousins, some

strays, all taking an unearned rest from their bus, tram
and motorbike journeys. The first star, that light that sig-
nals the start of the Sabbath, had long appeared in the sky,
even as we sinned on our various means of transport, but
we were never blamed for being late. When my Grandpa
appeared, looking pious in his Sabbath suit, it was a signal
for the meal to begin.

His name was Wolf, a savage name that had somehow
appended itself to the most gentle of men. My Grandpa
hailed from Poland, though 'hailed' would seem to over
dignify his passage. He ran, he fled; that frantic Jewish
bolt from a country drenched in mothers'-milk anti-
Semitism. All he carried with him was his portable
wealth, his father's sewing machine – and together with
his pride and his courage, he learned to make his living.
By the time he married my Grandma, he was an established master tailor. He rarely spoke about those early
days, and his old widowed mother, who later joined him,
forbade him to refer to them. She was a domineering
woman who, I was later told, had insisted on accomp-
anying her son and his new wife on their honeymoon.
With such information I began to entertain new thoughts
about my grandparents.

My Grandpa's workshop was on the top floor of the
house, and often he would let me play there with his
chalks and buttons. He spoke little but he smiled at me
and sometimes gently tuckled me under the chin. He
made no judgements, no demands, and I loved him. He
was a chain smoker of Black Cat cigarettes, and from
their packets he carefully saved all his coupons which he

would exchange for presents for his grandchildren. Our family present was a *Community Song Book*, and we often gathered around the piano, aunts, uncles and cousins, to belt out 'The Ash Grove', 'The Minstrel Boy', and 'All Through the Night'.

His button box was a treasure. Silver buttons, red, gold, blue, left-overs from his tailoring work during the war. For he had been given the sole concession in Wales to make the uniforms of American marine officers who were serving overseas. My Grandma welcomed the commission. Of her seven children, she had five daughters to shift, and little to speak of by way of a dowry. As it turned out, only one of the daughters fell off the perch – my Auntie Ray, the youngest and the most attractive. She landed in the arms of an American naval officer, impeccably fitted out in his new officer's jacket. His name was Ezekiel Woolf – my Auntie Ray might have been seduced by his surname – and she was forthwith swept off her feet to Boston, Massachusetts. She insisted on taking her sister Sylvia with her, and perhaps in the fullness of time, Ezekiel got two for the price of one.

That left to date three daughters on the shelf. One was my mother, Dorothy, or Dolly as she was called. Dolly was of a different cut from the rest of the brood. She was not, like the others, an early school leaver. She had endured a full and formal education and had qualified as a primary school teacher. She was a career girl and a suffragette to boot. In other words, Dolly was trouble, and as far as marriage prospects were concerned, my Grandma must have viewed her with despair. So when she suddenly

brought my father to the house, my Grandma did not
question his income or his prospects, she was just over-
whelmingly grateful.

Only two daughters left now, Beattie and also Annie
who she would keep by her for care in her old age. Her
two sons would find brides of their own, and though she
did not relish the role of mother-in-law she would do her
best to hold her tongue. It was the grandmother role that
she most looked forward to, and in my eyes as I grew up
she was a star.

My father's name was Eli Reuben. Like my grandfather, he had fled. Not from Poland but from Latvia, and
for the same reasons. Like Wolf, he had carried his
portable wealth. Two violins. One half- and one full-size.
Perhaps he hoped to make his living as a teacher. By various means of transport, he made his way across Europe.
His aim was Hamburg, the known port for ships sailing to
freedom. An elder brother, Israel, had already fled to
America and it was my father's purpose to join him there.
On reaching Hamburg, he had the misfortune of being
accosted by a dishonest ticket tout, who charged him for
a fare to America but put him on a boat bound for
Cardiff. Others who had fled were likewise swindled and
found themselves heading for Glasgow, Liverpool, Hull
and even Marseilles and Amsterdam. But the bulk turned
up in England, and the growth of the English Jewish
community at the turn of the century was directly due to
that consummate swindle that was practised in Hamburg
harbour. It did not take long for my father to realise that
Cardiff wasn't exactly New York, but there were many

others in the same boat, or rather just off it, a sorry group of misrouted pilgrims.

This was the only story that my father told of his past. Pre-Hamburg was clearly untellable and, as I grew older, I realised that had my father been stuck in Germany no memoir of mine could have been written. So my birthplace as well as my nationality were accidental, and I accepted that, by proxy, I was a survivor. It coloured my whole life, that concept of survival. It informs every aspect of my behaviour, and in later years every syllable that I write. But with it comes the burden of gratitude.

My father did gratitude in spades, and although he was naturalised and, apart from his difficulties with 'w's, spoke a perfect English, he never forgot his refugee status. And in that status, he included all his children. Every day he would remind us that we were guests in this country. It was like a mantra that orchestrated our childhood, and often it got on my nerves. But years later when he died and I stood by that six-foot plot of earth in which he was laid, I reckoned that at last I had a territorial right on the land that had welcomed my father and I didn't have to be a guest any more. Though I would gladly have forfeited that freedom in return for the gift to my father of more years. He was a mere sixty-eight when he died, and I hadn't yet grown to know him.

Of us four children, the eldest was Harold, and his status was clear from the start. A double status in fact, for he was not only the first-born, but a boy to boot. Then came my sister Beryl, who enjoyed the rank of first daughter.

When I arrived on the scene, I enjoyed the status of
'baby', and for two years I revelled in that spoiled standing. And then I was usurped. My brother Cyril was born
and overrode my rank. Now Cyril was 'baby' and I was
left statusless. That made me the outsider, a role unasked
for and often cursed.

We were not exactly poor, but we economised on everything. Clothes were passed down from the eldest to the
youngest, regardless of fashion, taste or even gender. We
did the same with instruments. The two violins that my
father had carried from Latvia were finally put to use. We
already had a piano, a piece of furniture that seemed a
given in a Jewish household, if only to serve as a stand for
barmitzvah and wedding photographs. But ours was
played, especially by Harold who seemed quite naturally to
consider it his own.

I recall that piece of furniture with great affection. Not
for its tonal qualities, which were painfully substandard,
but for its beauty of design. It was an upright Erard
piano, fashioned in rosewood. Two brass candlesticks
swivelled on each side of its front panel which was fretted
by thin wooden slats revealing a ruffled rose satin underneath. It was a joy to view. The keyboard was of
yellowish-white ivory, apart from one single note that had
turned blue in an otherwise healthy mouth. That note was
a middle 'D' and it was a useful marker, for an octave
above it was the first note of my favourite piece at that
time which I secretly picked out on that keyboard all
those years ago. Nostalgia is not necessarily related to
good taste. 'Minuet in G' by Paderewski is as daft and as

banal a piece of music as you could find. Though it was useful, that middle 'D', it worried me. I felt that with overuse it might fall out altogether like a rotten tooth, and I worried every time I saw my brother's heartless fingers treat it as if it was normal. So when he finished practising, I would soothe it and talk to it gently. I would lie to it, as was my wont, and tell it that it would get better. But as I recall, it grew progressively bluer.

Now that the piano ownership was settled, my father presented Beryl with the half-sized violin. He taught her himself and she showed promise. I did not like the sound of the violin and, mindful of the routine of clothes hand-me-downs, I dreaded that when Beryl graduated to a full-size instrument, the half-size would be passed on to me. I wanted a cello, but a cello was beyond our purse. So when my turn came I refused, and it was passed on to my little brother Cyril who ended up in the London Symphony Orchestra. Beryl too turned professional, and after playing in sundry American orchestras returned to Cardiff and the Welsh National Opera. Harold, the most talented of all of us, pursued a successful solo career. He was a prodigy, and my parents were not too sure how to handle him. By the age of seven he had exhausted all that the local teachers could teach him. The last of these, a Mr Leyshon from Cowbridge, suggested a teacher in London. He could go there on the weekends with little interruption to his schoolwork. My parents debated long and hard and finally decided that Harold's talent merited every chance. I remember telling middle 'D' that it could now have the weekends off, giving it time to recover.

The night before Harold was due to go to London I heard him crying in his room. There was nothing that I could do. He was proud and he wouldn't want it known that he was frightened and that he would be homesick. But my heart went out to him and I wished that he'd never had any talent. In the morning, we all trouped off to Cardiff station. We huddled together on the platform and I hoped that the train would never come. My father had arranged for Harold to be put under the charge of the guard, and when the train at last drew into the station the guard alighted and stretched out his hand. We were all reluctant to push Harold forward so the guard had to come to us and take Harold's hand. My mother bent down to kiss him but he turned away, his back to us, and I knew that he was crying. I watched him as he stepped onto the puffer train, his little case knocking against his bare leg and his young back firmly turned against his heartless family. I saw the sweat gathering behind his knees, homesickness already oozing from every pore, and I turned away. We huddled there while the train pulled out of the station, shivering with our guilt.

As the weeks passed, it became easier to let him go, and Harold himself seemed more and more anxious to leave. He came home with outrageous stories of his London life, of Madame Levinskaya, his teacher, and the crazy inhabitants of the boarding house that she owned. Of the audacious food she cooked, mixing pineapple, for example, with chicken. He felt very grown-up, very cos-mopolitan, and secretly he came to regard us all as provincial. My mother tried to keep him on an even keel.

But what worried her most was her son's growing attachment to his teacher, together with his scorn for our blue-toothed piano, comparing it to his weekend Steinway grand. He was growing away from us. I know my mother was upset but I thought she deserved it for sending him away in the first place. It was not until I was married myself, and with children, that I realised that she was not to blame. It was her role to take the rap for our small misfortunes.

My father made his feelings known to my mother, but at decision time he simply withdrew. It was not that he was a coward, he was simply shy and it was not in his nature to put himself forward. His temperament was that of a scholar. He immersed himself in readings of Jewish law and tradition and he loved to discuss the finer points of his readings with other friends who were similarly inclined. Discussion and debate were his natural bent, and had he been able to stay in his village he would have become a Talmudic scholar, with a violin for his hobby. But now, with a wife and four children, he had to make a living.

He became a tally-man, or packman as they called them in the valleys. Credit Drapery, its posh name, was a common pursuit among refugees at the time. Its advantage was that it required little initial capital. A friend who was already in the business would introduce you to a wholesale warehouse where you would buy menswear, shirts, socks and even suits, pack them and take your parcels to the mining villages of the Glamorgan or Rhondda valleys. A shilling a week was the usual deposit for goods, and often those goods would be worn-out before the final payment. Occasionally my father would waive the last payments. Even so, he managed to make a fair living. But he didn't graduate to the heights of the Great Universal Stores which started off in the same packman way. He had no business acumen, he was not ambitious. He simply acknowledged when enough was enough.

It was a hard grind. Every Friday, before our trek to Riverside, he would do his packing. I used to watch him, his meticulous folding of brown paper and the delicate knotting of the strings. Jews are very good at packing. They've had to run away so often, they've had plenty of rehearsal. Sometimes he would take me with him and I would help carry his parcels and wonder how he ever managed alone. He was much loved in the valleys. The miners' wives would be on their doorsteps waiting for him, calling his name, 'Eli, Eli', as he traipsed up the hill to their houses. And there was always a strong cup of tea for him with a Welsh scone. After his rounds and his collections, we would make our empty-handed way back to the station as the miners would be leaving the pits after their day's shift. You could hear them singing in the distance and pick out their harmonies and descants, engrained gifts which had required no training in counterpoint or harmony. The pits are closed now and the valleys are silent with not even an echo to be heard, and the community is disintegrated into the high rises that now sprout from their simple terrace homes. I'm glad my father did not live to see it.

*

When I was seven, I was released from the Tredegarville Infant School and promoted to Roath Park Girls' School. Beryl was already there and so was Harold, in the boys' department. We would take the penny tram ride up the City Road, but sometimes Harold would go on his bike and take me on the cross bar. I loved those rides. When we reached Albany Road, we would stop off at Woolworths, nip into the shop and steal a bar of Cadbury's chocolate. I would never have done that from our corner shop because I knew the owner who lived above the premises. But there was no flesh and blood dwelling above Woolworths so it seemed almost incumbent on me to relieve them of a little of their stock. We'd finish the chocolate by the time we reached school, clearly in a hurry to remove all the evidence. I could easily have grown up to be a thief. The fact that I didn't had nothing to do with morals; it had to do with cowardice. I was terrified of being caught.

I remember very little about my years at Roath Park, except that I was daily aware of the boys' department next door. It was this awareness, I suppose, that prompted my breast growth. Only pimples really, but I stuck them out with pride having achieved my first qualification for the downward spiral, and all the risks, excitement, joy and pain that that descent entails. But there was one memorable aspect of my Roath Park days. I began to read. Not the usual classics that baptise growing girls. I didn't go to libraries or children's bookshops. I had another source. A secret one.

It was the custom in those days among mining families

that the sons followed their fathers into the pits and the daughters were sent away to service. In his tally-rounds, my father made good friends with many families and it was from one of these that he chose Gladys to come to Cardiff as our live-in maid. My mother was not a home-body and she hated housework. Her time was spent working for Jewish charities; the blind, the old and the infirm. She was never to lose her reforming zeal. So Gladys came to live with us. She was seventeen years old, an innocent, and I loved her. She slept in the attic room at the top of the house, a large room which spanned the whole roof space and where I spent much of my child-hood. For Gladys's room was my idea of heaven. First there was the smell, or rather the scent. Evening in Paris perfume. Then there was Velouty vanishing cream and Pond's carnation face powder. On entering her room I faintly reeled in ecstasy. I'd take deep breaths and then sit beside her on her bed and she would tell me about her mam and dad and her brothers, Gareth, Gwyn and Euan. Gareth was her favourite, so naturally he was mine. After a while she would open a drawer and give me what she knew I had come for, the latest copy of *Peg's Paper*. Tuppence a week for the foundations of Mills and Boon. The magazine was full of romance. Love at first sight, fear of rejection, a jealous rival, a reconciliation and happy ever after. Proper stories that had a beginning, a middle and an end. And in that order. They represented the most pro-found influence on my future novelist's life. The aspect of a story, of simple narrative, still seems to me to be the least that a reader is entitled to, and I owe this opinion to

Gladys, her Velouty, her Pond's and her Evening in Paris. I took the magazine and hid it under my pillow. My samizdat. Once I caught chickenpox and I was allowed to sleep in my mother's bed. As my hand, from force of habit, wandered under the pillow I unearthed a book. I pulled it out of its underground and I read its title. *The Well of Loneliness* by Radclyffe Hall. I set to reading it but could make no sense of it. It was some years later that the word 'lesbian' found its meaning and I entertained new and astonishing thoughts about my mother.

I was coming to the end of my years in Roath Park and Harold and Beryl had already left for the high schools. In my last year, Cyril was released from Tredegarville, now it was my turn to take his hand on the tram ride to the big boys' school, and to hold his penny in my hot little hand. He was nervous. He'd never seen himself as a 'big boy'. He retained his childhood curiosity throughout his life. I feared he would be seen as an obvious victim, but I was proved wrong. It took him about a week to settle in. Then one day, after school, when I was waiting for him at the big boys' school gates, my pimples in proud projection, he came out in the middle of a little gang and walked right past me. I happily got the message, and thereafter he held his own penny, back and forth, on the tram down City Road.

Soon it was my turn for the big time. Cardiff High School for Girls. Beryl was already installed and leading the school orchestra and I had finally persuaded my mother to beg, borrow or steal me a cello. I asked no questions and I was happy to lug it on my back to the

house of Jenny Ware for lessons. The Ware family controlled the music industry in Cardiff. Herbert, the head of
the family, was nothing short of a pioneer. He was a violinist who had devoted his life to nurturing the musical
talent of whomsoever came his way. His wife Jenny was
the cellist. Winifred, the elder daughter, played the viola,
and Marjorie, the youngest, on whom I modelled myself,
played the cello. In time, I was sufficiently qualified to
join the school orchestra, though that was nothing to crow
about since our little band was far from philharmonic
standards. I was subleader of the cello section, which
meant nothing since there were only two of us, the leader
being Miss Horsfield the German teacher who was only
marginally more skilled than I. We made a smallish sound,
but it was quite terrible. Mr Price, the music master, was
our conductor and he despaired on his every beat. He
winced openly, but occasionally he would smile at Beryl
who was the only one in the band who could play in tune.
But we were a dogged crew and every Friday after school
we played together, and between us we managed to
murder 'Eine Kleine Nachtmusik' and 'Men of Harlech'.

Despite our Friday cacophony, I was happy at the
school. Except for our gym lesson, supervised by a sadist
called Miss Lewis. From the beginning she suspected that
I didn't take her work seriously and she punished me for
my lack of respect. She would give me detentions in the
gym and set me skipping till my heart stopped. And with
each turn of the rope I quietly resolved to kill her. Apart
from her gym responsibilities, she was in charge of checking our uniform, especially those items that were invisible

on our person. Thus she would ensure that we were wearing our liberty bodices, cotton knickerlinings and suspenders. For a discovered illegal garter she would happily have sent the wearer to the gallows, but she had to settle for two hundred lines. And our hats. Checking that the ribbon was clean and the elastic stretchable. Every morning she would stand at the school entrance and check up on our millinery. When I lost my summer panama I panicked. My mother refused to buy me a new one, so Beryl and I devised a strategy that would see us through the summer. We would walk together to the corner of The Parade, the school address. Beryl would go hatted to the school, borrow her best friend's panama, hide it under her blazer and scoot back to the corner. Then, both hatted, we entered the school, and I never failed to tip my borrowed hat to Cerberus at the gate.

Perhaps prompted by the panama incident, or in spite of it, I found myself suddenly conscious of fashion. I longed for nice clothes. It was my ambition in life to own a Burberry. My sights were painfully low. In my mother's eye, and indeed my own, a Burberry coat was equivalent to a mink. But I nagged for one, and nagged and nagged until Mom and Pop could stand it no longer. Pop was the first to surrender. Mom, on principle, held out a little longer. It was finally agreed that I could have a Burberry, but it had to be for life. And so to that end they invested in a coat that was at least three sizes too large. 'I'll shorten it,' Mom said, and she did. With her spirit of economy and my possible growth in mind, she did not cut the length. She folded it over. The hem came up to my armpits so I had, more or less, two Burberrys for the price of one. My mother was content; she had saved money. But the growth that she envisaged never materialised. I was a mere five-foot-one-and-a-half-inches when I first donned my double Burberry and I have remained five-foot-one and a half-inch to this day. The coat finally went to the Salvation Army and someone, somewhere, well over six-foot-tall is wearing that coat with an unpicked hem that will last him or her for a lifetime.

We had a friend at school called Celia. Not exactly a friend because Beryl and I did not like her very much, but we were supposed to be friends because her parents were friends of ours. We didn't like Celia because she was always thrown up in our faces as a paragon of virtue. 'Why can't you be like Celia?' Mom would moan. 'Celia never answers her mother back. Celia always puts her clothes away. Celia tidies her drawers.' We got so sick of Celia, Beryl and I, that we decided to turn her into a verb. 'Have you Celia'd your drawers?' Beryl would ask Mom, and that shut her up for a while. But at least Mom laughed. I don't think she liked Celia very much either.

We were good girls, Beryl and I. Beryl especially. She went early into good works and often helped my Mom in her charity pursuits. And she always did her homework. So did I, diligently, but I had sundry ways of doing it. I did it by proxy in Albany Road. Albany Road was the evening parade ground for girls like myself from Cardiff High and boys from the twin school in Newport Road. If you said you were going to Albany Road it was clear what you were going for. I would tell Mom that I was going to a friend's house to do my homework, to which she agreed, though she couldn't understand why such an innocent sortie necessitated a change of clothing. But no self-respecting schoolgirl would have been seen dead in her uniform on the Albany Road parade. So off with my liberty bodice, that quaint misnomer, that straitjacket of my childhood, and on with my one frock and petticoat and on to the parade, meeting friends whose mothers had been similarly conned. Just the one length of Albany Road and the return journey and, if we were lucky, a greeting to a high school boy, a pause, and a quick kiss in a shop doorway. We walked that parade only once in an evening. More than once would have threatened professionalism of the oldest kind.

I soon tired of Albany Road, having found a new source of interest. At five o'clock I would stand by my front bedroom window and watch the young boys returning from their shift on the docks. One of them in particular caught my eye. One day, he waved at me as he cycled past and thereafter I waited for him daily. I simply lived for his five o'clock wave. He was my knight on a two-wheeled charger, his hormones bursting at his seams. But it was that summer that I really fell in love. It was our custom every August to go to the seaside at Porthcawl. We'd stay in a boarding house a few steps away from Coney beach. The house belonged to a Mr Sidoli, who also owned the ice-cream franchise for the area. A daily cone for the family seemed to be included in our rent. That summer, Harold, Beryl and Cyril had gone to a music festival in

Bristol, so when my father was working I was alone with my mother on the sands.

The first time I saw him he was coming out of the sea, and I noted that he was skinny. But he looked sturdy and healthy enough and his leanness was obviously due to a metabolic rate of lightning. He stood on the shore for a while and shivered. I wanted to run to him and wrap my towel around his trembling body. All my life I have been troubled by this Samaritan urge, an urge which when spontaneous is a virtue but when premeditated can be a singular impediment, and over the years this predisposition of mine has done me few favours. But how was I to know all this in my twelfth year to heaven, lying there on the beach under Mom's constant eye, my budding breasts my infinite pride and Mom's sublime disturbance. I lay there and watched him. He seemed to enjoy his trembling, for he stood there and exhibited it with a certain pride, even as if he already sensed that vulnerability was a positive attraction. And for me it certainly was. I was hard put to stay where I was and not rush to his salvation. In any case, I would have been too late, for another Samaritan bore down on him and wrapped him roughly in a large towel. Then she folded him in a warm embrace and I knew that she wasn't a Samaritan. She was simply his mother.

The following day I saw him again. His family, like ours, always settled in the same spot. This time he was going into the sea, and I followed him. Mom's warnings orchestrated the length of my stroll to the water. 'Don't go out too far. Don't go out of your depth.' I was ashamed.

I looked around nonchalantly pretending that her voice was addressing somebody else. 'Mind the whales,' was the last I heard from her, and there was a waft of giggling around the beach, for in the whole thousand or more years of history of Porthcawl the only whales were made of papier mâché on the fairground.

He was standing on the shoreline, well within earshot of my Mom's last alarm. He looked at me and smiled.

'No whales,' he said. 'Only sharks.'

His voice was not yet fully broken. It was seductively fractured, occasionally whole, but now and then slipping into that perilous region that spelt manhood. In those days it took very little to lose my heart – I've become rather more picky since – but in that moment, in my twelfth year on Coney beach, against the raucous sounds of the fairground's figure eight, I fell in love, in real love, for the first time. And even without knowing his name or his provenance, I was more than ready to marry him. I shivered though I had not as yet tasted the cold surf. But that shiver of mine had nothing to do with the temperature. I was vibrating in the semiquavers of my heart's singing.

'Coming in?' he said.

I nodded. I did not trust my voice. I felt my Mom's eyes pierce my back. I dared not enter the sea's depth beyond her eye-line else she would be down on the shore screaming warnings of something far worse than whales.

'I can't swim.' I thought I'd better tell him.

'I'll teach you,' he said.

Even at barely twelve, I already sensed that the gates of

heaven were rarely open and that when they were it would be folly to dodge them. Bugger Mom, I thought, and I plunged into the sea beside him, and with brazen confidence I offered my chin to one of his resting hands, my midriff to his other as he balanced me face down on the water. I didn't want to learn to swim. I wanted to stay in his aquatic care for ever. I turned my head slightly to adjust to the cup of his hand and in doing so I caught sight of my mother on the shoreline. I prayed that she would hold her tongue. And she did. I was thankful that she was not wearing her bathing suit, but that didn't stop her from an investigative paddle. I noticed how she tucked her dress into her knicker elastic and waded through the water. I blessed her short legs, for I knew that dressed so, she could not come within apple distance of my Eden. She waded as far as her tucked-up garb would allow, then she stood for a while, bewildered. I gave her an innocent smile which must have reassured her, for she turned and made her way back to the sands. But from the back of her, stooped a little, she looked defeated, and in that moment I loved her with a burning and troublesome rage and I withdrew from my Eden with shame. He was surprised.

'Don't you want to learn to swim?' he asked.

'Not now. Tomorrow perhaps.'

I didn't want to lose him. I implied that I was still available to whatever teaching he wished to give me, and to secure some continuity I asked for his name.

'Percy,' he said. 'People call me Perce. What's yours?'

Now there's the rub. I hesitated. You see, I have problems with my name. I never know where the accent lies, whether on the first or second syllable. I tend to give both equal stress because I am loath to sell myself short. Some people give me three syllables. Berenice, *à la* Racine, but that seems to me to be over the top. Now I come to think of it, it's been a trouble all my life, not knowing how I'm pronounced. Mom and Pop called me Bern, which gave no clue at all. Perce was waiting, and I had to say something. So I looked him straight in the eye and gave him my two equal syllables.

'Ber-nice,' I said.

'That's a nice name,' he said.

'So's yours,' I told him.

I must have been deeply in love, for no one in a loveless mind would dream of considering Percy as a pleasant sounding handle, but at that time, the name made my young ears water.

I returned to Mom's side. She smiled at me with some relief, having reckoned, I suppose, that I'd not been gone long enough to lose my virginity, and for the rest of the day we were close to each other for whatever misguided or tortured reason.

That night I dreamed about Percy and about water. Warm water, soothing like a caress, and in the morning my limbs seemed to me like strangers. Indeed my whole body had taken on a sense of 'anotherness' and I knew that I had changed beyond recall. But it did not frighten me. I accepted that change as a wholly logical result of my Percy experience, and after breakfast I rushed to the beach for its renewal.

It was a Saturday. My father had arrived the night

before. During our August holiday in Porthcawl he came only at weekends. It was different when he was there, mainly because Mom was different. The constant eye she kept on me in his absence was now doubled, nay quadrupled, what with Pop's eyes on me as well. Mom's overheedfulness was no doubt for Pop's viewing, and his, no doubt, for hers. They were trying to impress each other and I was the target of their competitive caution. That Saturday, the beach was crowded. The weekend fathers helped swell the throng, together with the natives and the trippers who couldn't make it on weekdays. They parked themselves where they could, respecting those sites reserved for regulars who, after all, brought annual wealth to their town. Our sandy spot was empty, awaiting our occupation, as was Percy's holding. We settled ourselves, Mom and Pop in folding chairs while I lay on my towel beside them, my face to the early sun.

'Lie on your front, Bern,' Mom said. 'Get your back done.'

I knew she wasn't concerned with the evenness of my tan, she simply felt more comfortable when my woman's growth was hidden. She said it for Pop's sake too, knowing that his embarrassment was even more acute than her own. I turned myself over willingly for I found such a position more comfortable if I was to keep an eye on Percy's holding and joyfully anticipate its occupation. I must have fallen asleep because I was woken suddenly by a burning on my back.

'What's the time?'

I panicked, viewing Percy's site still untenanted.

'Twelve o'clock,' Mom said. 'You've been fast asleep.
I'm going in the water. Want to come?'

It would have been a relief to cool off, but that water
was mine. Mine and Percy's, and I didn't want anyone
else squatting it any more than I would welcome invaders
on Percy's sandy site. But Mom was already pulling me to
my feet and Pop was water-prepared too, his feet shod in
rubber shoes though there wasn't a pebble in sight. We
traipsed down to the water and I tried to feel part of my
parents' excitement, though no one would have thought it
seeing their grim faces as they tiptoed into the brine, inch
by dogged inch to their waistlines, squealing with each
cold step. Then they would wait an eternity before taking
the final plunge. I had dipped long before them, always
facing the shoreline, my wary eye on Percy's nest. I heard
Pop take the plunge and the thrashing of the rubbered feet
publicising his courage. Then Mom, ashamed, dipped to
her neck and let out an apologetic cry of minor achievement.

'I'm going in,' I said. 'I'm cold.'

I wanted to keep a closer eye on Percy's holding though
I knew that my proximity would in no way hasten his
arrival. As I walked back to our patch I was struck with
fear. Fear that I would never see him again. I had been so
happy the night before, but I was aware too of a shadow
of sadness, as if the corollary of joy was the possibility of
loss. I sat on the sand and stared at the spot where he
should have been, and my stomach turned over. A bunch
of natives, six of them – I knew they were natives because
I had seen them before, sitting in the dunes, away from

the beach knowing their August place – they were eyeing
Percy's place, skirting it slightly and then, with furtive
temerity, actually usurping that holy ground. They squat-
ted there, laying out their towels and picnicked – with a
proprietary right, as if the pitch had always been theirs
and ever more would be so. They scraped a hole in the
middle of the site and planted a union jack in the centre.
They might just as well have taken my Percy and buried
him, for I never saw him again. To this day, the cup of a
man's hand under my chin will ship me back into the seas
of my childhood and hold me there in blissful recall.

But at the time I was sorely bruised. I was angry too,
and that anger signalled the end of my innocence and laid
the seeds of that melancholy to which I seem occasionally
disposed. On the whole, I was an unhappy child, and not
an easy one. I stole, I swore, I lied and I sulked. My
mother said that all I gave her was aggravation, a word
that for many years I thought was Yiddish. But in whatever language, I knew it was not a filial gift of any kind. I
cannot even claim an abused childhood. My father never
suffered unemployment, my mother took in nobody's
washing, no uncle laid a finger on me and I was never
hungry. Yet I was abused. We all were, my brothers and
sister, by parental expectation. Such expectation is an
abuse of a kind. It didn't matter that it was motivated by
love, its effect was damaging and long-lasting. Even today,
my parents long dead, I ache for their approval.

I came to dread Sundays. Not all of them, only those
when my brother Harold was at home. When he was

away at Madame Levinskaya's, Sunday was a gentle day.
I would watch Pop as he took his time over his favourite
breakfast, his legacy from his home, his bowl of cream
cheese mixed with cucumber and sour cream, followed by
a salt herring which he would dice into succulent pieces.
Then he would place a cube of sugar in his mouth and
through it he would filter a glass of hot lemon tea. I think
he must have had an asbestos stomach, for the scalding tea
went down with relish and without pain. Then the day
would stretch quietly as we chose our own leisure ways
and waited for the prodigy to come home. But on some
weekends my Mom kept Harold by her, and those were
the Sundays I dreaded. Showing-off Sundays in the salon,
or rather the drawing room, where the piano was kept, the
violin stands, the music, along with all my parents' expectations. Mom would invite friends, making a point of
including Celia's parents. It's possible that she wanted to
let them know that there was more to life than tidying
one's drawers, which was possibly what their blessed
Pollyanna was doing at the time. Tea was served, home-
made cakes and biscuits and much was made of it so that
show-off time would appear incidental.

All the guests knew from long habit why they had been
invited, and one of them could always be relied upon to
ask Harold to give them a tune. Which he did, without
demur. I knew what he was going to play. He'd chosen it
for my parents. A piece which displayed his astonishing
technique. Liszt's 'Campanella'. I watched his fingers as
they buzzed like a swarm of bees, hovering over the keys,
magnetising them without touch. I was proud of him. I

knew he would have preferred to play a movement of a
simple Mozart sonata or an earnest Bach fugue, but he
was obliging Mom, and I thought he was kind. Though
why do I keep loading my mother with all that expectation? With hindsight I have gentler thoughts. It was my
father, that man whom I loved, that gentle self-effacing
man, it was he who supplied those goods of expectation. It
was my mother who simply delivered.

After Harold had done his filial bit it was inevitable that
Beryl should follow. She did not oblige with a show-off
piece. She played part of a Bach suite without accompaniment. And as she played the last chord I noticed how
Cyril, little Cyril, knowing his duty, took his violin out of
the case. It was always at that moment that I felt bypassed.
My cello playing was by no means ripe for the spectacle.
I remember the lump gathering in my throat and the
squeezing of my eyes to stem the tears. But I endured. I
endured every one of those bloody Sundays until I could
stand it no longer. I simply absented myself from the
parlour, went upstairs to my bedroom, sat on my bed and
cried. From below I heard the echoes of Cyril's 'Gypsy
Rondo' and I knew that my Mom would be pleased. I was
missed, of course, and shortly Mom came up to my room.
I expected her to be cross, but she was gentle with me.
She didn't ask what was troubling me. She knew full
well.

'Bern,' she said, and she held my hand, 'in a family like
ours, there has to be a listener.'

At the time, that gave me little comfort. But unknow-
ingly, perhaps, she was giving me a gift. She was offering

me a talent prerequisite for a writer, the talent of listening. She was giving me the *ear* to practise, for the ear needs rehearsal as well as any violin or piano, and I had plenty of that kind of practice in my childhood as I honed my ear with unconscious diligence.

A little while ago, when I was asked to talk on the radio about the music that I love, I realised how my choice was related to family and to nostalgia, first bred during those Sundays despite their having upset me so. My first choice was Beethoven's Piano Concerto Number Four. When he was only ten years old, Harold had played it with the Scottish Symphony Orchestra conducted by George Szell . . . It would be on the wireless, he told us. I asked him if he was frightened. 'Once I get over the beginning,' he said, 'I'll be all right.' I thought he was referring to nerves until I realised that the beginning of that concerto is possibly the most terrifying for any performer, for the piano begins clean, with no encouraging preamble from the orchestra that sits in silent judgement behind him.

Next I celebrated Beryl . . . When we were living together in London, I was woken every morning by the opening chords of the Bach Chaconne. It was my eight o'clock alarm call, and utterly reliable. I think even the cockerels depended on my sister. I immersed myself in her version, in her accents and her phrasing. Today, when I hear other violinists do it differently, I think they're wrong, and in one corner of my heart I shall always think so. That memory has less to do with interpretation than it has to do with simple sibling affection.

Cyril was my last choice. It was the Eisteddfodd season.

The set piece was the 'Gavotte' from the Bach Partita in E major. All over Wales, distracted mothers of aspiring Menuhins must have held their breath while their loved ones did or did not come to grips with the double-stopping. Every day I would listen while my little brother ploughed his lonely and sticky furrow. I knew exactly when he would stop and repeat. I anticipated his every mistake. I pre-heard his every sigh. To this day I believe his version to be the norm, and what they call the norm always astonishes me. Sometimes I listen to the Heifitz authorised version, and I don't believe a note of it.

I never let up practising my listening. But I didn't allow my Sunday nightmares to overshadow the pleasure of our Friday nights at Grandma's house in Riverside. My two aunts Ray and Sylvie had been slave-traded to America long before I was born. My gentle Auntie Beattie had been Shanghaied too, but only to Glasgow, in the grip of a man of the cloth. His name was Max. Though he led the service with fervour, he was never able to keep a congregation for long and he was shunted from *bima* to *bima*, throbbing with devout piety. Only my saintly Auntie Annie, the last of the daughters, remained unmarried, but her role as carer was proscribed. She never complained. It was in her nature to see to people. 'I'll see to myself when the others are seen to,' she would say. As the eldest child, she cared for her younger siblings. She would take her food when the others had eaten. She would wait for them to fall asleep before she would go to her bed. She would wait for their happiness before she felt entitled to her own, and she would have looked after their dying had she been able. In time, her role extended to the grand-children and I was one of the recipients of her caring. She was my constant and unpaid therapist. I am ashamed now that I was often tempted to pity her. But that was my unpardonable failing.

Of my Grandma's brood, that left the two sons, Uncle Hymie and Uncle Monty. Uncle Hymie was her favourite, and for him she had great expectations. 'He'll keep us all,' she would say. 'He'll be a doctor and he'll marry a rich girl from a nice Jewish family.' But Uncle Hymie did not oblige. He had no scholarship, no money, and to cap it all he married Leah. Leah was the daughter of a taxi driver and she hailed from London. In my Grandma's eyes, London was either Buckingham Palace or the alleys of Soho, and when Leah arrived for the family viewing, with her hennaed hair, black fishnet stockings and a rosebud of a mouth, Grandma knew that the House of Windsor was not in Leah's blood, and she dreaded to think what was.

That left my Uncle Monty, of whom there had never been expectations of any kind. In most families there is an elected member. A scapegoat. That was my Uncle Monty. Everybody knew of Uncle Monty's dubious past but nobody wanted to talk about it. Then one day he told it to me. He must have sensed that I wouldn't judge him. He had been part of a street gang dedicated to theft and the destruction of property. When he was sixteen he lied about his age and joined the army, which didn't knock any sense into him. All it did was knock into my uncle three large pieces of shrapnel, one in his head and two in his legs.

'I must have passed out,' he told me, 'and when I woke up it was dark and I thought I was blind. And there was a terrible smell. Familiar. I'd smelt it in the trenches on the Somme. I was dead, I thought. Just alive enough to smell myself. I felt around me. I was lying on a stone slab and I knew that I was in a morgue. I had to get out of there and I crawled to the door and started to yell. Then someone was pushing the door open, shoving me to the side. I must have passed out, but I heard someone say, "But you were dead yesterday". He sounded very cross.' Then my uncle laughed. 'Takes more than a morgue to kill me,' he said.

I warmed to him after that story, together with Auntie Sophie who discovered that she had become his wife. I did not treat him as an elected member, although at Friday night suppers he was still served the tail-end of a fish or the wings of a fowl. In the light of his swearing, his farting, his appalling table manners and his tempers, allowance had to be made for a man who had a steel plate in his head and leg and had dwelt among the dead.

It was spring, 1938. The daffodils stubbornly flowered in our garden though nobody had dead-headed them when they had last withered. That had been my job. While Harold and Beryl and Cyril were practising, I was appointed dead-header, hardly a career to be proud of. On a CV it would impress nobody. In no way could I put my heart into it, and thus I was neglectful. But there were more important issues than budding daffodils.

That autumn, long after the daffodils had sprouted and

died, the house was filled with rumour. And weaved into
that rumour was one whispered word. Hitler. And because
it was whispered, I regarded it as a swear word. My
Grandma had attached a Yiddish curse to the word which,
being translated, was a wish that a million boils should sit
on Hitler's bottom. At the time I was convinced that
Hitler was a swear word, one that I could add to my
growing bad words collection. I already had 'bloody' and
'damn' and 'blast', and it was Harold who contributed
'fuck'. He told me that Mom and Pop had done it four
times – he must have been as innocent as I – but I didn't
know what the word meant because I couldn't fathom
what the 'it' was that Mom and Pop had done. But I used
the word anyway, whispering it to myself along with
bloody, damn and now Hitler. I loved the rhythm of those
words and I strung them together ringing out defiance and
rebellion. So 'fuck bloody damn Hitler' would accompany
my detention skipping for the hateful Miss Lewis, or the
onesees-twosees ball game against the wall. At night I
used it as a prayer and I even tapped it out on the blue D
of our piano. Its colour seemed apt clothing for the words.

Terrible stories were rumoured from Germany. Jews
were being rounded up in every city. The Nuremberg
Laws forbade them to hold any official position. Then on
9 November came *Kristallnacht*, the night of broken glass.
Jewish houses, shops and synagogues all over Germany
were looted and destroyed. Thousands of Jews tried to
leave the country, but getting out was not easy. A heavy
blood tax had to be paid by each immigrant, and in those
countries prepared to receive them guarantees were

requested for their maintenance. But child refugees were exempted from these restrictions and so the *Kindertransport* began, the evacuation of Jewish children to foster families and hostels.

The floor of our drawing room told its own story. To my boundless relief it was no longer the salon. In any case, Harold and his 'Campanella' had been shifted to America and a new and renowned teacher. He would stay with his two hijacked aunts. He would concertise and make his mark. Now the floor was covered with clothes, shoes and boots, tools, books and satchels. My parents, along with other members of the Jewish community, were collecting. Collecting the wherewithals for the refugees who were trickling out of Germany. Few of the Welsh or English believed the terrible stories of their plight, and wondered what all the fuss was about. But Jews believed it, because many of them had been there before. Mom and Pop devoted most of their time to this collecting, doling it out to those who had already arrived and begging for money as guarantees. My Mom was rarely at home. She was out begging. And so was my Pop on a Sunday. Cyril, Beryl and I had the job of sorting the collection, labelling it according to size. We often wondered who would wear the clothes. We had never seen a real live refugee. Those who had arrived were housed in sheltered accommodation where they were taught English and helped on their way, dogged by fear for those they had left behind; their parents, their siblings and their friends. We wanted to meet them and make them our friends. Mom and Pop must have had similar thoughts.

It was a Friday, a day on which practising Protestants collected their *Church Times*, the Catholics their *Tablet*, and the Jews their *Jewish Chronicle*. The Friday fix for all. We were having breakfast when the papers were delivered. We heard the rattle of the letterbox and we all rose. But Pop got there first. There was the *Herald* and the *New Statesman*, and he put those aside. He held the *Jewish Chronicle* in his hand and placed it before him. It was a journal that catered for all tastes. If you wanted to know who was going to marry whom, or which boy would be prematurely jettisoned into barmitzvah manhood, or who had died or been born, you would find it in the appropriate pages. In the provinces round-up, you could discover how much money the Cardiff Zionist group had raised for refugees. And of course there was the general news. Most of it relating to Jewish topics, and all of it dire. Dire warnings of a possible second world war, fearful rumours of the fate of German Jews. In those winter days of 1938, long before the displacement of thousands of nationals all over the world, the word 'refugee' was synonymous with Jew. It needed no attribute, and in the Jewish community of Cardiff it was a buzz-word that hummed in every conversation. Every issue of the *Jewish Chronicle* printed a long and painful list in which German and Austrian parents pleaded for families to take their children, to somehow get them out to safety and to care for them. Pop opened the *Chronicle* to its centre fold and laid the spread on the table. Two whole pages of heartbreaking entreaty.

'Let's have a boy,' Beryl said. And I agreed. We were both of that hungry age.

'That's right,' Cyril said. He missed Harold terribly and he wanted to redress the balance. We pored over the paper.

'Look. There's one,' Beryl said. 'Franz. Tall, blue eyes, polite. He sounds nice Mom,' she said.

I spotted one called Hans, who was well-educated, friendly, tall with black curly hair. Cyril found one, a Peter who was a twelve-year-old violinist. Then Beryl found another, Paul from Berlin, sixteen, handsome, friendly, good-tempered. Talented painter.

'Let's take Paul,' she shouted.

Then Pop, who all that time had been silent, that mild-mannered man, rarely given to outburst of temper, banged his hand on the table. Confronted by so many desperate entreaties, he could not contain his anguish.

'For Chris's sake,' he shouted, 'this is not a marriage bureau.'

I felt ashamed, and so did Beryl and we said nothing. But the use of the word 'Christ', and out of my gentle Pop's mouth astonished me. I knew that in our house it was a swear word, but somehow I didn't think it qualified for my collection. I knew it would not sit well with 'fuck' and 'bloody'.

'Boy or girl, it's irrelevant.' Pop spoke softly now. 'So is age. So is behaviour. The only thing that matters is to save a life.'

Then he drew out a pencil from his handkerchief pocket. He stood up and closed his eyes and landed the pencil point on one of the pleas. He opened his eyes and read his choice. 'Save our son, Hugo,' it said. 'Fourteen.

Please.' A simple plea. No references, no attributes. An address in Hamburg was added.

'It's Hugo from Hamburg,' Mom said.

I noticed a faint smile that hovered on my father's lips. Perhaps he was recalling his waiting days in Hamburg harbour where he himself had qualified as a survivor.

It took a bit of planning, and many months of wading through red tape and bureaucracy. Pop made several journeys to Woburn House in London to acquire the relevant permits. At the same time he tried to pave the way for the release of Hugo's parents. The authorities gave him little hope of success. At last, in the spring of 1939, Hugo's papers came through, and the daffodils were again in bud. Pop went to London to meet this Hugo, of whom he knew nothing. He could have been of a good temperament or bad. He could have been friendly or hostile. His eyes and his hair could have been of any colour. All he had in common with those hundreds of applicants was the simple wish to go on breathing.

Pop later told us how he waited on the platform at Liverpool Street station. Many people got off the boat-train. He had no idea what Hugo looked like and he thought he would have to wait until all the passengers went on their way, except for one lone figure who would stand waiting. And it was then, on the almost empty platform, that he found Hugo. Their journey back to Cardiff was a silent one. Hugo spoke no English. My father tried Yiddish, and although it's possible that Hugo understood much of it he was still non-communicative. But he did smile sometimes and Pop had to settle for that.

It was late when they arrived at the house, but we had all waited up for them. My Mom took Hugo in her arms and held him for a while. He did not resist her embrace. Without a word, she took him to his bedroom and settled him. She knew that he needed to be alone. By morning Hugo had thawed a little, and over breakfast we taught him the words for everything on the table. He even laughed sometimes. My parents never relaxed their efforts to save Hugo's parents but no trace could be found of them.

Five months after Hugo's arrival, Germany entered Poland and the Second World War was declared. By that time Hugo was speaking a good English, but he needed no language of whatever tongue to learn that he would never see his parents again.

PART TWO

War was declared, but nothing happened. We were waiting for the bombs to fall. Cerberus still stood at the school gate. Her work load had increased. On top of hats, blazers and underwear, she was now supervising our gas masks – those little cardboard boxes that we shoulder-carried every day to school. In pre-war days the school organised random fire drills, but now they were called bomb drills and were far more exciting. No one took fire drills seriously, but bombs were different. A bell would sound and we would form orderly lines and troop down into the basement cloakrooms. Once there, we would put our gas masks on and wait for the bombs to fall. Since Miss Lewis was pernickety about order, and took time out to berate a pupil who was not exactly in line, the movement to the basement was often delayed, giving ample time for a bomb to obliterate the whole school before shelter could be reached. But for Miss Lewis, death and destruction was preferable to disorder. We were allowed five minutes of silent shelter and then we were filed back to our classrooms. During those minutes, none of us were recognisable. Our gas-masked faces were uniform. There was no beauty to envy, no ugliness to pity, and I thought that a gas-masked world would be a happier place. But still the bombs didn't fall.

Until one night the Splott steelworks were hit and Mom and Pop decided to move us out of the terrace. We would all go to Riverside and live with my Grandma. It seemed a pointless move, since Grandma's house was in a direct line to the docks, as obvious a bombing target as were the steelworks. But at least the family would all be together, was Mom's rationale. Grandma was now a widow. Grandpa had died of Black Cat addiction a year before the war, but he'd left a palpable presence in the house. His workshop remained untouched and his clothes still hung in the wardrobe. 'It makes me miss him less,' Grandma would say. Once I caught her crying into his suits. Apart from the togetherness of family, there were other advantages to the move. Grandma was an able homemaker and cook, and in her hands our sparse food rations seemed to stretch much further. Besides, she kept a few chickens in her back garden and occasionally there were extra eggs. Even with a mean sugar ration, she could still bake her Sabbath biscuits and sweet rolls.

My Auntie Annie, who normally would have been part of the domestic scene, was now rarely at home. The war had brought her true happiness. For the first time in her

life, and at a ripish age, she had fallen deeply in love, a
love that was eagerly returned. As a girl, she had trained
as an auxiliary nurse, though that career was curtailed by
the pressures from home. But now, in spite of Grandma's
disapproval, she volunteered her services to the Women's
Auxiliary Corps and took her rusted skills to the first aid
depot close to the docks. It was there that she met Jim, a
volunteer in the Home Guard responsible for those
injured in the bombings. He rode a motorbike and every
day he would call for my auntie and settle her on the pil-
lion. I watched them as they drove off together, her arms
around his waist, her face creased with smiles so long
withheld and now, with reason, released for the first time.
We were all happy for her. Even Grandma, though she
was at pains to hide it. For she felt she should disapprove
on principle. Jim was not Jewish, which was bad enough.
But worse was that he was a married man with grown-up
children. And not even widowed. But few of us gave
much thought to Mrs Jim. Years later, when I myself
became a Mrs Jim, I regretted my lack of concern for her.
But at the time I saw that her errant husband was making
my Auntie Annie very happy and on her behalf I remember wishing that the war would last for ever.

There was only one disadvantage to the Riverside
house. It lacked a cellar, and as such there was no means
of shelter. The council had offered to build an Anderson
shelter in the garden, but that meant losing the chickens,
so Grandma turned the offer down. But shelter was at
hand. Very close at hand. Next door in fact. But that was
the rub. My Grandma was not on speaking terms with her

neighbour. Never had been. Mrs Price's house was number forty-two, the last on Brook Street. Her garden wall overlooked the River Taff, the river that necklaced the city. Mrs Price was of no account, Grandma said. Though in terms of money, Mrs Price accounted for plenty, for her house was a brothel. There were about five steady girls in residence, and men of all shapes and sizes were seen to come and go. Lately there had been some sailors among them, and the odd soldier. The war was being good to Mrs Price, which in no way improved my Grandma's temper.

One night, Cardiff suffered a serious air raid. It seemed to signal that many more were on the way. Cardiff's turn. We checked our blackout curtains, and huddled together in the kitchen. Cyril, Beryl, Hugo and I were sent to crouch under the table and our sole view was of Mom and Grandma's hosiered legs and Pop's brown spats. Three nights a week Pop was on fire watch duty, but that night was not one of them, and we were glad that he was with us. Whatever happened, we would suffer it together.

We listened as the siren faded and we waited for the bombs to fall. We had hardly settled in our places before a resounding bang set the house a-shiver. We heard a loud crash of glass that seemed to come from the front of the house and as the noise settled Grandma's cockerel crowed in the garden, rudely awakened and thinking that it was morning. We clung together. We were frightened, and as we saw three hands reach under the table we knew that the grown-ups were frightened too.

'We must get out of Cardiff,' I heard Pop say.

I wondered why he hadn't thought of such a move before. Then there was another bang, more distant this time.

'They've hit the docks,' Grandma said, as we listened to a series of loud droppings.

'That poor Levy family,' Pop whispered.

The Levys were friends. Mr Levy had hailed from the same Latvian village as Pop. He'd arrived earlier than my father, and had set up a chandler's shop on the Bute Road, the main highway to the docks. The family lived above the shop which brought in a good living. Pop prayed that they were safe.

'I'll go there tomorrow,' he said.

We waited for the sound of more droppings but all we heard was the roar of planes overhead and the offended spluttering of anti-aircraft gunfire. We heard the distancing decrescendo, and we waited till all was quiet. It was some time before the sound of the all clear released us. We could hear the singing from next door, a triumphant 'There'll always be an England' echoed through our floor boards, men's and women's voices. Grandma stamped her feet, not so much to quell the noise as to express her frustration. None of us moved. We knew that our windows had been smashed and we were loath to view the damage. It was Pop who made the first move.

'We're alive,' he said. 'Let's thank God for that.'

We followed him into the front rooms. The windows of both the dining and living rooms were smashed and shards of glass covered the carpets and furniture.

'Let's clear it in the morning,' I said.

'We'll do it now,' said Grandma. 'Tomorrow is a new day and we'll start again.'

It was the middle of the night, but it was my Grandma's house and it was her decision. We set to work and in an hour all was cleared. We boarded up the broken windows.

'We'll get a glass man tomorrow,' Grandma said.

We were too excited to sleep, but there was no question of missing school the following day. We sat down to breakfast at eight o'clock as was usual. Pop had already left the house. He'd tried phoning the Levys in the docks but all the lines were down. He did not expect the dock trams to be running, so somehow or other he made his way through the rubble. Soon after he'd left, my Auntie Annie returned from duty. Her face was flushed from whatever duty she'd been busy at.

'What a night,' she said, as the flush turned to blush.

Grandma poured her a cup of tea. First things first, no matter what her daughter had been up to.

'The docks again,' Auntie Annie said between gulps. 'Twenty-five dead, they say, and they're still counting. We haven't stopped all night.'

Stopped what? we wondered.

'I've got to get some sleep,' she said. She finished her tea and rose from the table.

'Don't you want something to eat?' Grandma asked.

'I ate at the canteen,' she said.

She was on her way to her room, anxious to avoid further questioning, and I wished her good rest, dreaming of her various duties and looking forward to the night's pick-up.

We were just about ready to leave for school, the four of us, when the doorbell rang. Grandma said it was probably the man for the glass who was wont to wander in the area for post-bombing work. I answered the door. I knew it was Mrs Price, even though I'd never met her. But I had imagined her and she looked exactly as I had envisaged. She was not dressed for early morning. Perhaps she had not been to bed, for she was formally dressed in loose, blousy attire that sat comfortably on her large frame. Her make-up though, had been removed, and a bluish and heavily veined nose suggested a taste for the bottle. I smiled at her. Even if she was of no account, as Grandma had declared, I wanted her to be my friend. I welcomed her.

'You're just in time for a cup of tea,' I said, and I hoped that Grandma would oblige. I led her into the kitchen. I didn't bother to announce her. I knew she was known. I watched for my Grandma's reaction. She was at first surprised, then confused, but mindful no doubt of Mrs Price's cellar, she gave her a faint smile. And even the offer of a cup of tea. I more or less pushed Mrs Price into the seat I'd left and Mom put a cup before her.

'Terrible night,' Mrs Price said. 'I'm sorry for your damage. My windows have gone too.'

'Only some of our windows,' Grandma said.

She was not going to be cowed. She would weather the bombing, she seemed to be saying, even without a shelter. Mrs Price leaned forward. Her blouse dipped her cup of tea but it didn't trouble her. She had blouses galore.

'Why don't you come next door when it happens again,' she said. 'You'll be safer there. Just knock when the siren goes. I'll let you in.'

'That's very kind of you,' Mom said, seeing that Grandma didn't know how to respond.

'We're neighbours after all,' Mrs Price replied.

Then Grandma thawed. 'You're very kind Mrs Price,' she said.

'Call me Bertha.'

'Bertha,' Grandma repeated, for even a woman of no account was entitled to a name. 'There are seven of us, mind,' she said.

'You're all welcome. We'll just have to squeeze in,' Bertha said. She gulped what was left of her tea and went back to her business.

Eventually we were ushered off to school. Hugo went in a different direction. He had opted to go to a technical establishment where he could learn a trade. He'd chosen carpentry, anxious to make a living and to repay Mom and Pop for his rescue. His survivor's guilt was compounded by gratitude, an uneasy load which he was to bear all of his life.

The tram ride took us through the city centre. There was no sign of damage. The docks were the target and the civic centre, the museum and the university were over-flown. I had hoped that one of the pilots might have hesitated over Cardiff High School for Girls, but as we approached, Beryl and I, we sadly found it intact, and Cerberus at the gate. She didn't even look tired, and she performed her guard duties with meticulous care, able to take her time since, on that day, there was clear absenteeism.

My first lesson was Geography, with Miss Launder. Nobody liked geography, but Miss Launder liked it well enough and it was her enthusiasm that kept us awake. But that morning she seemed to have lost her zeal. I remember studying the world map under her direction, pointing out the many pink bits, our British Empire of the past, but indifferent to our colonialism I fell asleep and was wakened only by the bell that signalled the end of the lesson. Others were woken too, and perhaps even Miss Launder herself, for I saw her stagger out of the door with her atlas awry. Our French lesson was next and we waited for Miss O'Reilly. And waited. Then Miss Rhys came in, our headmistress, and announced that in view of absenteeism, due to last night's raid, she was going to close the school for the day and urged us to go home and get some rest. 'Let's all pray that we have a peaceful night,' she said.

But I had no intention of praying for a quiet night. I wanted to sample Mrs Price's cellar and all the forbidden fruit therein that Grandma had threatened. That night, though, it was London's turn, and Birmingham the next, and for the whole of the following week we were left alone. But Cardiff's important, I kept saying to myself. I couldn't understand why we were being so neglected. As it turned out, it was not neglect. It was build-up. We were going to be attended to. And with a vengeance.

It came on a Saturday night. When the siren sounded we trooped next door. Mom, Pop, Cyril, Beryl, Hugo and

I, with Grandma reluctantly in the rear. We were fortunate. It was not Pop's duty night, neither was it Auntie Annie's. But she had gone to the pictures, with a friend, she had said. Mrs Jim must have been told that her husband was on duty. We were not particularly worried. We guessed that the steelworks or the docks were the targets and the city centre of cinemas would be overflown. But Hugo was anxious. He had grown close to Auntie Annie. By nature, or more likely by circumstance, he was a reticent boy, wary of showing his feelings, and of all our family Auntie Annie was the only one allowed to touch him, to hug him, and on occasion to make him smile.

'I told her not to go out,' he said. 'It's not safe at night.'

'She'll be all right,' I assured him, though with no reason. 'They'll be going for the docks,' I said.

Mrs Price herself answered the door, and rushed us quickly towards the cellar steps.

'Bit crowded tonight,' she said, 'but there's still room.' She led the way.

Since the space was underground and windowless it was brightly lit. The front half of the room, beneath the outdoor grille, served as the coal cellar, and that area was sealed off with a metal door. The rest of the space could well have passed as a sitting room, for it was carpeted and comfortably furnished. Along each of the three walls, there was a bench covered with flowered padding. In the middle was a table sporting a linen tablecloth, on which lay cups and saucers of the best china, thermos flasks of tea and coffee and plates of cakes and sandwiches. Mrs Price's sundry connections must have included the gift of food coupons. Grandma was relieved that she had brought a contribution, and she handed over her bag of home-made biscuits. We were all set for an underground picnic.

The room was pretty crowded and nobody seemed to take much note of our arrival. The laughter and chatter was not interrupted, but they did move up on their benches to make room for us. We didn't all sit together, we were scattered, and I was glad of it for it made me feel like part of the Price family. I found myself sitting next to a woman who told me her name was Alice. She did not ask for mine, for which I was grateful. My name problem still dogged me. She went on chatting to her neighbour which gave me an opportunity to look around and examine my company.

Apart from my own family, there were eleven in all. Seven women and four men. Two of the men were young soldiers and they blushed and hid their faces. I think it was the presence of Grandma that unnerved them. She must have reminded them of their mothers. The other two men were Pop's age, or thereabouts, very smartly dressed, and they looked rich. I wondered if they were married. All the girls wore dressing gowns, but not of towelling or rough cotton. They were silk and patterned, and clearly the uniform of the house. I eavesdropped on their conversations. The suits were telling the dressing gowns of their pre-war holidays in Paris. The girls giggled and the soldiers looked into their laps. My family sat in silence, though I don't think in judgement. They simply felt very out of place. Mom and Grandma wore fixed smiles. Hugo looked anxious and Pop was simply pretending he wasn't there.

Mrs Price rapped the table and there was silence. She turned to Grandma and explained.

'When we're in the shelter,' she said, 'we always say a little prayer. Please join in if you wish.' She folded her hands on her ample lap and the women and men followed suit. Mom, Pop and Grandma, suspicious of what was to follow, shifted into neutrality.

'The Lord is my shepherd,' Mrs Price began, then my family, reassured, folded their hands on their laps. It was a psalm after all, and from our own part of the bible, the old testament, with its guarantee of no mention of Jesus. So we all joined in the twenty-third psalm. Except for Hugo. His English was not yet good enough to master all the words, but he knew it well enough in German and he could not resist joining in, whispering in his mother tongue. Beryl, who was sitting next to him, kicked him on the shins. In such a shelter any language on earth would have been preferable and, as if in sardonic acknowledgement, we heard the first bombs fall.

'The docks,' Mrs Price said, whose acute ear could gauge distances. The echo of the sound was remote enough for safety. 'Who's for tea or coffee?' she asked, as if she were hosting a party.

Pop was glad that the Levy family had moved out of the docks. They had evacuated themselves to the countryside and Pop harboured thoughts of doing the same. He would come back to Cardiff for his three-nights-a-week fire watch duty, assured of the safety of his family.

The women helped hand out the cups to the gathering. The bombing continued, but its distant echo did not faze them. They struck me as being so polite and friendly, and though I thought that what they were doing for a living was very very naughty and very very rude, I couldn't share Grandma's opinion that it was immoral. They were simply offering a service. I was glad to see that Grandma's biscuits were going down extremely well and I saw her smile as the plate emptied. Perhaps it marked the beginning of a Mrs Price thaw.

There was a lull in the bombing, but we could still hear the anti-aircraft fire as the planes flew overhead. 'They're on their way back,' one of the possibly married men said. And with some relief, for the thought of being found dead in a brothel was faintly unappealing. His wife would no doubt understand. She was too understanding by far, and of course it was her unbearable decency that had landed him in a brothel in the first place. But no sooner had the man spoken than the house itself reverberated with an offended shudder, in the echo of a bomb that seemed to have fallen, if not as a direct hit then at least on next door. Mrs Price and my Grandma looked at each other.

'We're done,' they both said.

'But at least we're safe,' said Pop.

We were all quiet then, with nothing to do or say but to listen helplessly to the staccato bomb drops that seemed to be peppering our very neighbourhood with annihilation.

'We're safe though,' Mrs Price whispered, as if she didn't want the Germans to hear.

'So far,' one of the soldiers said. He would have felt safer on a battlefield.

There was a lull once more but we did not trust it, until we heard the clanging bells of the fire engines and ambulances and we found comfort in the fact that we were not alone. We waited for the all clear and dreaded it too, for it would signal the time to discover all that we had lost. When it came Mrs Price stood up. 'Back to work, girls,' she said shamelessly. Even possibly homeless, she still had to make a living. But her clients had lost their appetite. Grateful for their lives, the urge for anything else on earth had quickly evaporated. Mrs Price led the way up the stairs and the punters followed, pushing in front of my family, anxious to escape. They were not interested in joining the chorus of 'There'll always be an England', which traditionally celebrated survival, and the women themselves lost interest in the song. They too were anxious to get out of the cellar. They made their way to their rooms as they had been ordered, but the men followed Mrs Price into the street; if there was still a street, then they would rush off to their homes and their billets, and feign surprise at the damage in an area which they had never in their lives frequented. But we were hanging back anyway, afraid of what we might find.

'We're alive,' Pop said again, and he led the family towards the stairs.

We were all thinking of Auntie Annie, not daring to wonder if we would ever see her again. But no one mentioned her name. We would keep her alive in our silence. Once at the top of the stairs we viewed the ground floor.

It was still there, though not quite as we'd left it. The plate glass panelling of the front door lay shattered into a mosaic on the doormat, though the word 'Welcome' was still discernible.

'All right girls?' Mrs Price called up the stairs.

'Still there,' one of the girls called. 'Just broken glass.'

Then, satisfied that she wouldn't be homeless, Mrs Price gingerly opened the door that opened on to the street. Which was no longer there. Still more or less intact, was the side that housed Grandma and Mrs Price and three others that reached the corner. But the opposite side of the street, that had been a row of a dozen or so polite terraced houses last evening, was now a scattered heap of rubbish, glass and concrete. Rescuers were already digging for survivors. The punters ran for their lives, but we were rooted to the spot outside Mrs Price's door. I remember feeling ashamed; ashamed that I had prayed for Cardiff to be seen to. Now I saw the flesh and blood of my wishful cravings, especially the blood, and I felt that I had killed these people with my own hands. But I was selfish. I wanted to be evacuated to a safer place.

Pop crossed what was left of the road to lend a hand, and in doing so he decided to find a place in the countryside. The rest of us still did not move. We were silent. Grandma seemed unconcerned about viewing the damage to her own home. The unspoken name of Auntie Annie creaked in the silence that would hold her safe. We watched a convoy of ambulances cross the bridge and turn down the road that skirted the river. We waited until they had passed our house and we still waited there in a

silence that outscreamed the ringing of bells and the racket
of hammers and shovels on the concrete. And then, on the
bridge, taking its savouring survival time, came a lone
motorbike, one we knew by nightly sight, but mostly now
by heart. Hugo, standing by my side, who'd never been
known to shed a tear, now broke down, sobbing uncon-
trollably, sobs laced with the laughter of his relief. Auntie
Annie, whose name we now yelled aloud, was coming
home.

Jim slowed the bike to a stop outside Mrs Price's door
then, unwilling to face a comment of any kind, he rushed
over the road to help in the rescue. Auntie Annie had
hardly dismounted when Hugo, that reticent, impassive,
phlegmatic almost-brother of ours, ran to her side and
hugged her to make sure that she was real. We asked her
no questions. It was enough to see her alive, and by the
same token she asked none of us but came towards our
group and embraced us all, an astonished Mrs Price
included. We heard the rattle of the tea trolley over the
bridge. 'There'll always be an England,' Mrs Price sang,
and there always would be, it seemed, as long as the tea
trolley rolled along.

'I think we all need a drink,' Grandma said, and I was
astonished. It was so un-Grandma a remark. She was not
a drinker and I doubted that there was any alcohol in the
house. And probably no glasses anyway, because from the
outside the house looked totally defenestrated and certainly in no state to hold a cocktail party. I think Grandma
was simply drunk on the sense of survival, for she trembled as she said, 'There must be many dead across the

road'. She led the way into the house. She had no care of how it looked.

'I'm going to see if I can help,' Hugo said.

Auntie Annie took his hand and together they crossed over the rubble to Pop's side. I felt I should help too, but I'd never seen a dead person and I was frightened. So it was only Grandma and Mrs Price, Mom, Beryl, Cyril and I, who entered the house to drink to our survival.

The front rooms were strewn with glass.

'No more glaziers,' Grandma said. 'We'll board up the windows and wait until the war's over.'

'You're right,' Mrs Price said. 'It's not worth it.'

We went into the kitchen. The dresser was still intact but its contents littered the floor. My Grandma's beloved collection of jugs lay shattered but she did not even sigh. She handed me a sweeping brush. 'Sweep it all into a pile, *bubbele*,' she said. Then she opened a cupboard and brought out two bottles, miraculously unbroken. There were no glasses left but she found some cups and laid them on the table, the table that had been our pre-Mrs Price shelter. One bottle was half full. It was Palwin's No. 4, that oversweet Kosher wine left over from our last Seder meal at Passover, ten small drops of which we used to mark the plagues that God had visited on Pharaoh. The other bottle was vodka. Grandpa's. Like Pop he had relished his Sunday breakfast, his reminder of home. But instead of Pop's scalding lemon tea, Grandpa had washed down his salt herring with vodka. I missed him. The Black Cat cigarette smell of him, his quiet smile when he pinched my cheek. He was such a still and retiring man, taking up so little space in our lives, yet the hole he had left behind was immeasurable.

Grandma poured from the Palwin's bottle. I noticed that the vodka was not on offer. We drank, sipping quietly in the silence and the shame of survivors.

The following day Pop made enquiries about a possible place of shelter. Somewhere in the countryside, not too far from Cardiff so that we could still go to school. It took him only a few days to find a place and to make arrangements. It was a farm a few miles out of the city, about a quarter of a mile from a little train station that ran a regular service into Cardiff. The farm was owned by two unmarried ladies who put it about that they were sisters. They were happy to rent out the main farmhouse and to move themselves into the barn alongside. And so we shifted ourselves. All of us except for Grandma, who refused to leave Auntie Annie. No amount of persuasion could move her. 'We've got Mrs Price,' she kept saying. 'We'll be safe.'

We were not too worried. We would visit every day on our way home from school. And we took little with us. We did not envisage a long stay. We were evacuating ourselves as a formality, but at heart we found the move faintly ridiculous. For Jews are not countryside people. They don't have the right clothes. They are landless and urban. An English country farmer envisages lineage, and territory that would be handed down from father to son. Jews are by nature displaced, impermanent, and do not enjoy the privilege of constant legacy. By a historical imperative, their living has to be made on the move, and

what they leave to their children must be portable. Every
year at the Seder table, Jews raise their glasses of Palwin's
No. 4 and say, 'Next year in Jerusalem'. But they have no
intention of going there, or even a wish. It is but a nod to
the Promised Land. Their true home is exile, and the creative energy that that exile engenders. But that does not
include the countryside. For that grey area they are ill-
equipped. Fauna and flora faze them. They can get by on
flora perhaps. They know a buttercup when they see one,
a daffodil, a rose, a lily. But fauna floors them. They can
only begin to understand fauna if they think in terms of
food. *Cholent*, for instance, is a dish which, among orthodox Jews, is prepared on a Friday before the Sabbath and
left overnight in the oven to cook. Basically it's a beef stew
with beans, and it's usually unappetising. Of late, it has
become an 'in' dish, a sort of Jewish cassoulet. Its essen-
tial ingredient is beef, so in the Jewish eye *cholent* is cows.
By the same token of cuisine, fish is chopped herring, and
chicken is chopped liver. And horses? Well, horses are for
Cossacks.

Thus, so pathetically green, we made our way into the
countryside. We had to dodge a few cows on our way to
the front door of the farm. The 'sisters' were at the gate
to greet us. Apart from that encounter, we saw nothing of
them during our stay. They kept themselves to themselves and went about their farming business. I was sorry
I saw so little of them. By that time I had understood the
matter of the *Well of Loneliness*, but I'd never encountered
the flesh and blood of it. I don't know what I expected to
find, but now, since I have grown up and mended my

ways, I am ashamed that I expected to find anything that was untoward.

Over the next few days we settled ourselves and tried to feel at home. Every morning the four of us walked to the station and took the train into Cardiff to go to school. We didn't always go together. Beryl was an early bird, so were Cyril and Hugo, but I was a lazybones and often had to run the quarter-mile to catch the train. Sometimes I missed it, but however late I was I could be sure that Miss Lewis would be waiting for me at the gate. I didn't care, I had grown bold. I no longer had to fear detention. The war had put a stop to all after-school activities. Even our weekly massacre of Mozart had been shifted to the afternoon. And I never bothered with the lines she handed out. I told her that my revision for the Lower School Certificate, GCSEs today, left me no time for trivial things and besides, I reminded her, there was a war on. There was little she could do except report me to Miss Rhys for insolence, but I think that Miss Rhys must have seen my point, for thereafter poor Miss Lewis left me alone. She had at last shut her mouth, a slim advantage to be reaped from the war.

Most days I called on Grandma on my way back to the station. She always had a cake for me. Baking was her pleasure. 'I miss you all,' she'd say, and I'd say the same. I wondered why we'd bothered to move at all. At night, we'd watch the bombers comb the country sky on their way to Cardiff docks. We felt safe then. It was when they were coming back that we were nervous. Nervous of their offload. And indeed several of their surplus bombs fell in fields nearby, shattering the farmhouse windows and frightening the horses. One of the homebound bombers flew into cloud, a cloud that turned out to be Caerphilly mountain, and we heard the crash and saw the fire in the distance. 'His poor mother,' Mom said. She dreaded those return runs. 'We might as well have stayed in Cardiff,' she would say, and I knew it would not be long before we upped sticks and took our chances in the big city. So as a child I equated the countryside with two attributes: its pointlessness and its impermanence. In other words, I didn't take it very seriously. But we stuck it out in that farmhouse for almost six months, and during that time I underwent a radical change. A change both of heart and of mind. I was not aware of it at the time, but with hindsight I know that that six months turned my vision around and allowed some room for thoughts unurban.

It all started one morning when I was leaving for school. Mom was standing by the window. Since our deurbanisation, she had spent an inordinate amount of time at windows. She was watching a lone cow, our *cholent*, wandering across a distant field. 'I wonder where that cow is going,' she said, 'and when it will get there.' Now my mother was a woman with a practical head on her shoulders, and I thought for a frightening moment that the countryside had finally sent her round the bend. I was too stunned to respond. The purpose of a cow's wanderings, and the estimated time of its arrival, had never given me cause to wonder. I knew where I was going, which was to school, reluctantly, and that if I didn't leave soon I would miss my train. And that morning, I did miss it, because I took more than my usual time to reach the station. I dawdled on my way. I even made frequent stops. My mother's wonderings had unnerved me. In Cardiff she would never have had such a thought. It struck me that in Calcutta she would have had a full-time wondering job. We had no visible cows in Cardiff, but there were plenty of ambulant animals, dogs and cats, and through a window glass, darkly or otherwise, she would never have wondered where they were going. I had no doubt that the countryside was getting to her, and I was not sure that it was beneficial.

I caught a later train and sneaked into school during assembly. But all day I couldn't concentrate, and after school on my way back from the station I found myself studying the hedgerow flowers; the red campion, the wild briar, the deadly nightshade, and devil's bit scabious, names I didn't know at the time, and finding pleasure in their discovery. When I reached the farm a smell, pleasant yet unfamiliar, wafted through the barn door, and on entering the kitchen I found my mother baking bread. Now in Cardiff she would no more bake a loaf than wonder about a wondering cow, and to cap it all, she had on her face a look of such radiant and peaceful pleasure that I had never seen in our city kitchen.

'I saw some pretty flowers in the hedges today,' I said. 'I wish I knew their names.'

'There's a flower book on the shelf,' she said. 'Let's go out tomorrow and see if we can name them.'

Thereafter everything in our country life changed. We

took walks every day, Mom and I. At first we said little to each other, as was our wont in the city. In any case, city subjects were beyond discussion. Homework neglected, drawers untidied, piano and cello unpractised, all these topics were best covered with silence. And unspoken they seemed more threatening. But in the country, these subjects were not only unworthy of discussion, they seemed to be absolutely irrelevant and merited no priority. In comparison, the destination of a cow seemed far more pertinent. As the days passed, we identified each hedgerow flower, our mouths choc-a-bloc full of unurban vocabulary. We watched birds and savoured their newly discovered names. When autumn came, we actually saw the leaves fall and watched them in wonder, a sight never witnessed in the city where autumn spelt leaves on the ground, unrelated to the beauty of their fall. At night, when the bombers had quit the skies, we looked up at the stars and whispered Orion and the Plough and the Bear. And when the snow fell, we saw our first robin that wasn't on a Christmas card. I have never been closer to my Mom than I was during that country sojourn.

When we returned to Cardiff, we slipped back into our urban silence and into the sham priorities of exams and tidy drawers. But often Mom and I would smile at each other as we recalled that rural magic, that sane wand that tapped everything into its right and proper place. And even now, so many years later, and urban-riddled, I can still watch a dog wandering in a crowded street and wonder where it is going.

*

We sat out the rest of the war in Cardiff. But not all of it in my Grandma's house. We moved; we went posh. Well, poshish. We moved to Penylan. At the time, with the war still raging, property was cheap. Pop was no businessman, and it was Mom who persuaded him to take advantage of the fall in prices. Penylan was the habitat of the upwardly mobile, a phrase that in a lifetime could never be applied to Mom and Pop. Mobile they might well have been, in respect to their history, but upward was a word that implied greed and ambition, neither of which attributes could be applied to my parents. But Penylan was undoubtedly that kind of district. It was but one step away from Cyncoed. If you could manage a house in Cyncoed, you could mobile no upwarder. You had arrived. But we had no intention of climbing. We moved into 101 Kimberley Road, Penylan, and we stayed there. Mom and Pop died in that house and Beryl, having moved back from America in 1979, still lives there. Over the years, Cyncoed got its comeuppance and gave way to Llandaff, Radyr and Llanishen. But Penylan has neither sunk nor swum. It never had ideas above its station, and thus it has held its independent own.

It was a terraced house, joined by a hydrangea bush to the Thomases next door. We woke the street up with our practising, but nobody complained. Both Beryl and Cyril were destined for a professional music future. And I'd found a new pleasure in the piano. Now that Harold was away, I was no longer ashamed of my shortcomings and, unlike the cello, the piano was impossible to play out of tune. Besides, by that time we had a new piano, a Rogers upright. Harold had won it at an Eisteddfodd competition when he was ten. Today it is played by his grandchildren. Its keyboard was pristine white. I missed the blue note on our old Erard, that rogue tooth which by now must have crumbled into decay. We'd left it behind at Glossop Terrace for the extended maternity use, possibly to lullaby the new babies to sleep. The 'salon' days were left behind too, and parental expectation now focused on exam results so our homework was strictly overseen. Hugo too was subject to their expectation, though they had less rights on him than they imposed on their own flesh and blood. I know that they were motivated by love, but they saw us not as individuals but as extensions of themselves. They could not bring themselves to let us go. Later on, with my own children, I learned that letting go is the hardest goal for a parent to achieve. Try as I would, I could never wholly relinquish that hold. I learned that holding on is a disguised path to self-fulfilment. I have rarely met a parent who has happily achieved that separation.

It was under this burden of expectation that I worked for my Higher Certificate. I had done well in the lower grade, very well in fact. But enough was never enough. Mom was disappointed that I hadn't done better and lost no time in making it known. I knew I couldn't win, no matter how well I acquitted myself. I plodded on regardless, aching for her approval. I thought I might have earned it with the result of my Higher Certificate exams. I'd achieved good grades, with a distinction in English. It was the custom of the Welsh Education Board to award a State scholarship to a pupil who'd gained a distinction. A

State scholarship meant Oxford, and such an award had
been the Board's custom for years. But God is occasionally not good, and that year, his back was turned. The
Board passed on State scholarships and in their stead
awarded special exhibitions to their own universities. Mom
said that she was very disappointed in me. So go fight
City Hall.

So it was that I showed up at Cardiff University and
embarked on my first major folly. I decided to read
English. I was not to know it at the time, but to be satu-
rated in the great nineteenth-century tradition of the
English novel turned out to be no great favour to a would-
be writer. To have George Eliot at your elbow and Jane
Austen breathing down your neck is a faintly resistible
proposition. In my own time I would have read their
works anyway, without being stifled by an English degree.
I would perhaps have regretted *Beowulf*, that I wouldn't
have read in other circumstances. *Beowulf* was the sole
bright light in my course. For a couple of years I had
Beryl for company. She was reading German, though she
didn't know why. She muddled through, and when it was
over she joined ENSA, the war-time entertainment unit,
and she fiddled her way through the tommy camps in
India. Cyril was still at Cardiff Boys' High, struggling
with his exams between playing cricket and the violin.
Hugo had been awarded an apprenticeship in a furniture
factory in Cheltenham, so there were only the two of us at
home. Despite the war, I recall it as a peaceful time.
Cardiff suffered its share of air raids, but our district was
overflown. Mom and Pop were still caring for refugees,

trying to ignore the horrendous rumours that grapevined from secret German sources. 'Gas' was mentioned, and 'crematoria'. The most benign whisper was 'ghetto'. That was a word that they could deal with. The word was historical, it was known, and though it implied deprivation, it was not necessarily fatal. So they said 'ghetto' aloud, for the other words were beyond whispering.

They worked tirelessly for those refugees who had managed to escape, and they compiled a register of those of their kin who were missing. It was their intention to find them when the war was over, or at least to discover what had become of them. Though what with the grapevine rumours, they already knew.

I was glad that they were busy with other people, that their expectations had been transferred elsewhere, for it left Cyril and me off the hook. I was glad too that their concern and hope could extend beyond the family and that others qualified for their expectations. Mom's disappointment in me could now find new targets, and I went about my university course no longer aching to get a first but simply to get by.

It was in my third and final year at university that I was fallen in love with. The object of my unrequited affection was one of my tutors. He was a man of the cloth, whose expertise centred around decadence in Jacobean drama, a subject which I thought sat uneasily about his collar. I too was interested in that theme, and that was the basis of our connection. I was flattered of course, but I was aware that on his part his feelings were a little more than academic, and I wondered how to handle them. I thought I understood what had attracted him. Like many a pious man, and human after all, he was excited by the concept of degeneracy, the core of sin. In those days I was degenerate enough, scruffy, bohemian, anarchic, and he couldn't wait to lay his healing evangelical hands on me. Moreover, he was a High Church man with unshakeable opinions on who was responsible for the death of his Lord. I was a Jew. His pet Jew. Not bad for starters. In his eyes, I was utterly taboo. I was close to the devil and, like the devil, I confess that I tempted and teased him, and then withdrew. I confess too, ashamedly, that I enjoyed my stratagems, but always with a modicum of guilt, wondering whether somewhere in the background lurked a Mrs Jim. There were presents, books, Mozart recordings, all of which I callously accepted. I had thought of staying on for another year to pursue a B.Ed. course that would qualify me as a grammar school teacher, but the non-affair was too confusing for both of us and I decided to forgo further education and seek my fortune in the wider world. I managed a two-one degree, disappointing my tutor as well as my Mom, and I decided it was time for me to leave Cardiff.

The war showed little sign of coming to an end. Schools were desperately short of teachers, especially boys' schools, with staffs depleted by those masters serving in the forces. So despite my lack of a B.Ed., I had little difficulty in finding a post at a prestigious boys' grammar school in Birmingham. It was not a city that I would have deliberately chosen, but that choice was secondary to the need to leave Cardiff, to draw a line under that troublesome, exciting and sometimes dramatic period of my life, and to start anew.

Mom, Pop, Hugo and Cyril came to see me off at the station. Mom cried as if I was going to the North Pole. And Cyril laughed. Between those two expressions I knew that I would be missed, and that I too would miss them. But I would do more than miss them. I feared that I would find myself unanchored.

Handsworth Grammar School was part of a poor, run-down district in Birmingham. Petty crime was rife, and hooliganism. But it was a friendly area, and its humour even made the appalling Birmingham accent fairly tolerable. I loved teaching. There's no greater joy than being able to turn a streetwise yobbo into a lover of poetry. I started with Wordsworth and had them read it aloud, which they did, initially with embarrassment and then with growing bravado and pleasure. I particularly loved teaching grammar; clauses, the main and subsidiaries, the subjects and predicates, and especially parsing, techniques that find no place in present-day curricula.

During my time at the school, I was introduced to Gilbert and Sullivan and helped produce *The Gondoliers*. Since then I've become an aficionado, one of the few benefits I reaped from my Birmingham stay. But there was one major drawback. The headmaster. He was a Reverend Walton, a man of the cloth. Now I'd had problems with the cloth before, and certainly it had had problems with me. But the Reverend Walton did not fancy me. The devil had already seduced him long before my arrival. Every morning I would pass a line of frightened young boys queuing up at the headmaster's door. Some of them came out weeping, and others holding back their tears. I discovered that early mornings were Reverend Walton's caning sessions. None of the other staff seemed to find it exceptional. I was outraged. I began a lonely crusade. I visited parents and over a few months I was able to muster a parents' protest committee. Word came to the cloth's ear, and he was far from delighted. I waited to be summoned to his study. He lost no time in calling me to account, although I wasn't actually called to account for anything, and I was allowed no explanation, no discussion, no attempt to change his views. I was summarily dismissed. Fired. But for one reason or another, with a superb reference. I didn't bother to fight it as I would have found few allies. But I was angry. Many years later I put the Reverend Walton into a novel, *Sunday Best*, but I made him much worse and thus I leisurely vented my spleen.

The war was over. I thought of returning to Cardiff, but I knew that that city held no answers. So I made for London.

I often go back for reasons that I don't bother to understand. Recently I went home – I still call it home despite the fact that I haven't lived there for over fifty years and have a home of my own. I was once again homeward bound to attend a Welsh literary festival. I drove over the Severn Bridge, a span that was absent in my childhood. Once on the other side, I am greeted by a notice in a foreign tongue, which the authorities had had the grace to subtitle. 'Welcome to Wales', it tells me. Once upon a time, I had thought that the land was mine. But now I am made to feel a foreigner. It was so different when I was a child. Cardiffians were an ambivalent people, nervous, and with an unsure identity. Because of their proximity to England, they would cock an envious eye over the river Severn to the emblem of the rose, which was a far more seductive proposition than that of the leek. The Welsh nationalists of the north harboured a great mistrust of us hybrid dwellers in the south, while at the same time the English insisted that Cardiffians were Welsh. So we were ambiguous, equivocal, double-tongued. We didn't know where we stood, and our not knowing generated a certain excitement. It offered us choices. Exile or home. Now those choices have been withdrawn – the notice at the end of Severn Bridge has told me so. Cardiffian I may well be, but I am Welsh and I'd better believe it.

There are more reminders as I approach the city where I was born. Streets that I knew by heart are now labelled in a foreign tongue. Like Bottom in *A Midsummer's Night Dream*, my former person has been translated. But despite the streets' foreign tagging, I know my way well enough and even blindfolded I can trace the house where I think I might have been born. The communal garden that used to front it is now a car park and only one tree remains, a sycamore in the corner, shedding its offended leaves on the Volvos below. I stand in the space that number nine Glossop Terrace once occupied and I think of my mother. She died some years ago at the splendid age of ninety-four, and the day afterwards the council razed my

birthplace to the ground. I stand there, recalling the
house, room by room, staircase by staircase, landing by
landing, and the shiny slide-down banister that, without
interruption, linked the four ghost-filled floors. Around
the corner there's the Tredegarville Infant School. Or
was. But now it's a car park too. I wonder where all the
infants have gone, and whether for convenience's sake
they have turned into Minis and Ford Sierras. Then up
the City Road to higher things and the big girls' school,
which served what I was told were my needs until the
Eleven-plus. A penny tram ride it was, but sometimes I
would walk and spend the penny on humbugs from the
corner shop, where fat Beti wouldn't ask for sweet
coupons. The shop is still there, so is the school, but the
trams don't run any more. Woolworths has gone too, that
prep school for larceny. A supermarket has replaced it,
and you could no more leave an unlocked bike outside
than you could leave a safe door open. Albany Road has
changed too, that evening parade ground of mine. Now
there are no free hideaway doorways. The homeless have
taken them over, and for nothing more exciting than
sleeping. Not even a faint echo of a schoolgirl kiss lingers
on the graffitied walls.

Cardiff High School for Girls is my next port of call. A
proper grammar school it was. It's still there. At least it's
not a car park. It's a polytechnic now, and no doubt in the
fullness of time it will be calling itself a university. But
whatever it's called, a Miss Lewis of sorts will still be
standing at the gate. But there is a university proper in
Cardiff. It still stands where it was and it still functions.

It's part of the splendid civic centre, and it looks exactly the same as it did all those years ago. So does the Museum of Wales and its enviable art collection, and the theatre which now houses the Welsh National Opera. And the parks around the white-domed City Hall. None of these have changed, and suddenly it doesn't matter that every tag is subtitled in English, for music, art and theatre are what they are anywhere in the world, and in whatever language.

I pass the castle, and make my way to Grandma's house. I lean over the bridge and remember how every summer we would watch the Taff Swim, cheering the unknown bobbing heads. They don't swim there any-more. The Taff is too tired and too polluted to rise to high tide. In any case, it is now overlooked with a certain disdain by the vast Olympic pool built for the 1958 Commonwealth Games. In walking distance is the Library and its great reference section where I discovered the magazine *Horizon* and read T. S. Eliot for the first time. I was excited by his poems and I would read them over and over, sometimes aloud, which coloured their meaning. And not always to their advantage. The 'Jew' bits dis-turbed me. I have tried to find a literary justification for them, but in vain. Eliot was plainly a rabid anti-Semite.

Close by, where the market place once traded, stands the new St David's Hall, with the best acoustics in Europe. A Welsh achievement, in any language. I wander down to the docks. In my childhood, it was a salubrious and unsafe area. Tiger Bay was at its hub, and if you valued your person you did not stray there. The war-time bombing did for the docks area. There isn't a Tiger Bay any more and the docks are idle. The area has now become the 'in' place to live. The Chelsea harbour of Cardiff, with its posh restaurants and boutiques and its built-in ghetto of Somalis to lend it ethnic colour. And all of it labelled in Welsh.

My leaving visit is to the cemetery where Mom and Pop are buried. Bones. Bones. That magnetic pull. My permanent anchorage to the land where I was born. I read the Hebrew inscriptions on their tombs which require no translation.

I drive back to London and once more cross the Severn Bridge. Shortly I am greeted by a road sign which reads, 'Welcome to England'. And suddenly I feel a foreigner.

PART THREE

I have lived in London for over fifty years, but I still regard myself as a tourist. I've had myself photographed outside Buckingham Palace, the Tower of London, the National Gallery (taking in Trafalgar Square), St Paul's and the Millennium Eye. I have an album of such photographs that would not shame a Japanese woman who wishes to prove that she had visited London. But I think that I am proving it to myself. London was a childhood dream of mine and it seems now to be a dream unending. I am glad of that, for despite those fifty odd years I am simply passing through, in transit as it were to another exile.

Beryl had already settled in London by the time I was pushed out of Birmingham. I had saved only a little money and I had no job. After my Birmingham experience I had little confidence in the teaching profession, and I didn't relish returning to the classroom. I needed a job that would give me some pocket money and a free place to live. I was lucky. Beryl had already gathered a circle of friends and many of them were musicians, among them Ivry Gitlis, a young Israeli violinist with a talent already recognised and celebrated. He had left home to escape an over-expectant and demanding mother, and had found shelter with one of his many girlfriends in a flat a few doors away. He suggested I go and live with his mother as part companion and part 'lady's maid'. That was his mother's phrase.

I duly presented myself at Ivry's mother's apartment. Hedva and I took to each other immediately.

'I want you should be my lady's maid,' she said.

I nodded eagerly, though I had no more idea of a lady's maid's duties than Hedva herself.

'You should comb my hair,' Hedva said, primping it.

I had little idea how to comb my own, and my pathetic attempts were all too visible. I know that the just-got-out-of-bed look is now fashionable, but I blazed that trail over sixty years ago.

'You should also make up my face,' Hedva added, although she could see that my own had never known powder or lipstick.

I agreed, but we were game playing, each of us, and both of us knew it. But Hedva repeated the phrase.

'You will be my lady's maid,' she insisted.

She loved the expression. She simply wanted to be entitled to the phrase. It didn't have to entail any authentic practice.

So it was that I became Hedva's 'lady's maid' for three months, and during this time her hair remained uncombed and her lovely face unpainted. Though she had little money, she was deeply extravagant. She spent an inordinate amount of time on the telephone, usually to send telegrams to her friends and family in Israel. She assumed that the switchboard operator was illiterate and insisted on spelling out every letter of each message. 'H for Happy,' she would yell, 'A for Apple,' and so on through every single letter of 'Happy Birthday to You'. I would wait for the 'O's. Hedva's 'O's were a classic. She was plainly hooked on phonetics, and when the 'O's came she would adjust the mouthpiece and scream, 'O for LOndOn'. God knows what garbled message the Israeli child received, but however it was worded, it was laced with Hedva's love and lunacy.

Hedva lived in Belsize Park Gardens, and during my stay there I would wander up and down all the Belsizes, the Crescent, the Avenue, the Park, the Grove, the Square and the Lane. I loved the area, and it was my ambition at the time – my sights were still painfully low – to live in every Belsize available, and over the next year I did so, moving from bed-sit to bed-sit.

Beryl lived a short walk from Hedva's in a basement flat in Lambolle Drive, a mere turning off Belsize Square, so it was Belsize enough. Having satisfied my Belsize cravings, I moved in with Beryl who had a spare bed. After the war she had returned from her ENSA travels, laden with incense, sandals and Indian artefacts. She'd had her fill of 'The white cliffs of Dover', 'It's a long way to

Tipperary', 'Danny Boy' and 'All through the night', and she was taking lessons at the Royal Academy with Max Rostal, one of the finest teachers of the day. Beryl was a diligent pupil, and it was during this period that every morning, without fail, I was woken by the opening chords of the Bach Chaconne. My alarm clock, and a perpetual reminder to get myself a job.

I was no longer worried that Mom was disappointed with me, because I knew that she had more pressing problems on her mind. The stories that were coming out of Germany no longer slithered along the grapevine but were openly and obscenely exposed; the camps, the ovens, the gas and the six million. A search for survivors was under way, a search feared to be futile, but pestered by stubborn, unquenchable hope. There were various avenues of inquiry. There were refugee committees in all areas, busy with the urgent compilation of the names of those known to have perished, the millions of them, and those displaced persons of numbers unknown. One source of information was more direct. There were several news-sheets that specialised in refugee matters, and they contained advertisements seeking the whereabouts of lost relatives and friends. Mom and Pop scanned these regularly. Not on Hugo's behalf; it was already known that his parents had died in Auschwitz. They scanned the columns on behalf of those other refugees whom they had helped to escape.

I was home for the weekend on one of my many trips back to Cardiff. I liked to spend time with my parents and Cyril, and in any case I needed a break from my Chaconne awakenings. Cyril had won a place at the Royal Academy of Music, but that place would have to be held for him. He was due to be conscripted and he was waiting for his call-up papers. There was no chance that he would be sent to a battle zone, but Mom worried for him. He was still her baby after all.

We were playing a Mozart sonata together when I heard Pop shouting.

'Look at this,' he called from the kitchen.

We joined him, both of us. Mom came in from the garden. Pop was excited.

'Look at this,' he said again.

He was holding a news-sheet and he spread it out on the table. He pointed to an item.

'Read it,' he said.

It was Mom who obliged.

'Seeking the whereabouts of Hugo Gross of Hamburg, aged about twenty. Liesl Weissbort, 27 W49th Street, New York.' Mom read it all in one excited breath. 'We must ring Hugo,' she said. 'Perhaps she's an aunt, or a cousin, or maybe just a friend.'

It took some time to get through to him. Hugo lived in a boarding house, on the top floor, and he'd had to get down to the hall to pick up the phone.

'Hugo,' Mum shouted as soon as he answered, and she told him about the advertisement, reading it out once again. 'Who is this Liesl Weissbort?' she asked.

But it seemed that Hugo had no idea. The name was not familiar to him.

'We'll write to her anyhow,' Mom said. 'When can you come home?' she asked. 'We miss you.'

Then Cyril took the phone. 'Hugo,' he said, 'I've been called up. Take a few days off.'

Then it was my turn. 'This Liesl woman might be very rich and she'll want to marry you,' I said. But Hugo didn't laugh. He found very little to laugh about. But clearly he was intrigued by the advertisement.

'Find out who she is,' he said. Then there was a long pause. 'I'll come home soon.'

Mom wrote immediately.

'I could go and see her,' Pop said.

He'd been trying to arrange a passage to New York. He wanted to see Harold. The war had enforced a separation. Mom and Pop missed him terribly, but only one fare to America was possible. Pop would go on his own.

I decided to hang around in Cardiff for a while, at least until Cyril was called up. And I hoped that there would be a reply from the mysterious Liesl. It came, promptly and by express airmail. I noticed that Mom handed the letter over to Pop, signalling that the situation was now in his control.

'Read it to us,' she said.

Pop opened the envelope very carefully and slowly, for he was clearly nervous. He spread the letter on the table. It was one long page, fully covered with type-written script. Totally legible, offering no excuses for pause or hesitation.

'Dear Mr and Mrs Rubens,' Pop read. 'I was absolutely overjoyed to receive your letter and to know that Hugo is alive and well and is being cared for. You must wonder who I am. I am not a relative, and apart from Hugo's father, I was unknown to his family. For in truth, I was Hans Gross's mistress for twelve wonderful years.'

Pop simply had to pause. He looked at us all.

'How will Hugo take this?' Mom asked.

'He won't find it funny,' Cyril said. 'You can be sure of that.'

'You never know,' Pop said. 'These things happen,' and I wondered what my father had been up to.

'Go on,' Mom said.

'We were very discreet,' Pop read, 'and Greta knew nothing about it. Theirs was a happy enough marriage, and they were devoted to Hugo. I knew that he had left on the *Kindertransport*. I shared Hans's agony at having to let him go. In late August 1939, I learned that the Grosses had been taken, along with the other Jews in the same apartment block. Hans had often persuaded me to escape, but as long as he was alive I would not leave him. My own parents had already been taken and when I heard that Hans too had gone I knew that I would never see him again. So with the help of friends, I managed to leave Hamburg just before the outbreak of war. After a while, through devious routes, I finally reached America. My father's sister lived in New York. She was widowed and of substantial means. Then two months ago she died, and since she had no children I was her sole heir. I have never forgotten Hans, and am desperate to find any link with him. I would be overjoyed if Hugo would wish to join me here. I can give him a wonderful home, and prospects of work if he should wish. Perhaps he could just visit, and then make up his mind if he wants to stay. I

would of course pay his passage, and any expenses that he
would incur. Please let me know his wishes soon. May I
conclude by thanking you for saving Hugo and for giving
him a home. You would have had Hans and Greta's eternal blessings. Yours sincerely, Liesl Weissbort.'

We were all silent around the table. Then after a while
Mom said,

'It's up to Hugo. It's his decision.'

When the phone rang so early in the morning, we
sensed that it must be Hugo.

'If that's Hugo,' Mom said as I reached for the phone,
'say nothing to him. We must wait until he comes home.'

It was indeed Hugo, and he sounded very low.

'What's the matter?' I asked. 'You sound miserable.'

'I'm sick of this job,' he said. 'It's not getting me anywhere. I'm coming home.'

'Good news,' I said. 'We miss you. Don't worry. You'll
find something better.' In America, I thought. His job-
lessness would ease his decision.

'I've got to go now,' he said. 'Give in my notice, I'll let
you know when I'm coming.'

'Good luck,' I said. 'See you soon.'

I reported our conversation. They all thought it well
timed.

'Do we advise him?' Pop asked.

'Only if he asks our opinion,' Mom said. 'I think it's a
great opportunity for him, but I don't want to say so. We
can't guess his reaction to the letter.'

'It'll upset him,' Cyril said.

Hugo came home the following day. He was apologetic.

He felt he'd let my parents down. But they assured him they only wished for his happiness. Hugo raised an eyebrow at that word. It was foreign to him. Over supper, Pop told him that the Liesl woman had written. He handed him the letter.

'You may wish to read it on your own,' Pop said.

'Why?' Hugo asked. 'It can't be bad news. I know that they're dead.'

Mom put her arms round him. 'Read it,' she said. 'Whenever and wherever you like.'

Hugo opened it right away. I watched him carefully while he read. The news of his father's adultery was half way down the page and I waited, fearful of his reaction. And then he did the most astonishing thing. He smiled. Hugo actually smiled and the smallest hint of a chuckle escaped him. We were all relieved.

'It's not a bad idea,' he said when he had finished reading. 'I think I'd like to try it. If you don't mind,' he added. 'Just to try it,' he said. 'I can always come back home.'

'Never forget that,' Mom said.

'We can go together,' Pop said. 'I'm going to see Harold.'

'It will be wonderful to see him again,' Hugo said. His spirits were uplifted. He was almost excited.

Over the next two weeks, arrangements were made for their passage. And during that time, Cyril was called up. He was ordered to report to a barracks somewhere in Warwickshire. We saw him off at the station, from that same platform that had seen me leave for Birmingham, Beryl for India and a tearful young Harold for London.

Now my little brother was leaving too. Little Cyril, now almost six foot tall, laughing as always, because he had to, so moved was he by Mom's tears.

'I'll write,' he said. 'I'll let you know where I'm going.'

My mother hoped it would be somewhere in Wales, in weekend-leave distance from home. So a few days later when Cyril phoned she was devastated to learn that he was being posted to India. They were going to Liverpool for embarkation and he wanted me to meet him at Lime Street station and bring his violin. Mom was distraught.

'There's no fighting there,' I tried to console her. 'He'll see the world. It'll be like holiday. I think he's lucky.' But I would miss him, that little brother of mine who laughed away his fears, his caring and his pain.

I carried his violin to Liverpool, feeling a fraud. For I was not a musician, though I dearly wished and still do that it had been my choice of profession. He was waiting for me on the station platform, a toy soldier, barely recognisable but for his apologetic smile. I hugged him and was loath to let go. He had no time to spend with me. He had to get back to barracks.

'Two whole years,' I said.

'It won't be that long. Six months, I've heard, then I'll be home. But don't tell Mom.'

I handed over his violin, and in return he gave me a parcel.

'My civvies,' he said.

He kissed me shyly, then he left, slinging his fiddle over his shoulder, his legitimate weapon, and looking every inch a musician.

I caught the next train back to Cardiff. I gave a detailed account of our meeting and I said how handsome Cyril looked in his uniform. Then I handed over the parcel. Mom opened it and gently laid out his flannel trousers, his white shirt, his socks and his sandals, and then she broke down completely. It was as if she had four sons in the merchant navy, all reported missing. But I felt sorry for her. All her children had fled the nest, and because she had never been an earth mother their departures, laced with guilt, had been the more painful.

It was time for me to return to London. For the first time since he had been my half-brother, I kissed Hugo and wished him a good journey. I had spent all my parting grief on Cyril, so I had little feeling for Hugo's departure. In any case, I felt sure he would tire of New York soon enough and would return home. As I kissed Pop, and sent my love to Harold, I realised for the first time how much I was missing him, and like Mom I wished that all of us would come home again and be together as a family. I wished that Grandpa hadn't died. I wished there'd never been a war. Then I recalled that Auntie Annie had found love, and I had discovered the names of hedge flowers. And Hugo had been saved. Thus I comforted myself. But I was only twenty-two years of age and it seemed that I was too young to be counting my blessings. Such a pursuit was a form of abdication. I had to get back to London and find myself a job.

There was an A. S. Neill school in Hampstead, a progressive establishment that catered for the children of up-market parents who were too busy up-marketing to care for their children. As a result it contained a rag-bag of pupils, some very bright, some late developers, most of them delinquent and all of them unloved. There was no form of punishment in the school and pupils were in no way obliged to attend classes. Truancy was a meaningless word. It was so different from the Birmingham Grammar that it appealed to me. I applied to the school for a job. The interview board was made up of most of the staff and a handful of pupils, young and older, who were entitled to have their say as to my suitability. On the whole they found me satisfactory enough. My one drawback was my degree. A university degree was not considered a beneficial qualification for teaching at an A. S. Neill school. Rather it was an impediment, involving much academic baggage that was seen to be a burden in a progressive school. I told the Board that I attached little importance to it myself. Somehow I convinced them, and I was appointed.

I was nervous on my first day. In view of the voluntary nature of attendance I expected an empty classroom. But it was full, and I ascribed it to the pupils' curiosity. I learned that throughout the school there was no absenteeism, classes were fully attended, and I realised that the teaching was exciting enough to hold their attention. I loved the school. I was paid very little, but it was enough to underwrite my share of our flat where Beryl still Chaconned her life away.

Things were peaceful. Pop had returned from the States with glowing news of Harold's concertising, Hugo had opted to stay in New York and was content there and Cyril was stationed in Lahore. He was a stock master, in charge of kits and blankets. He wrote home like a tourist on holiday. Mom was peaceful. She had broadened her charity work and was now involved with SSAFFA, an organisation concerned with the welfare of the families of soldiers, sailors and airmen. Pop still sold in the valleys, but by now he had a car, a little Morris Minor, into which he packed his parcels and, in first gear, he climbed the steep hills of the Rhondda. But Mom still needed something to worry about. Cyril, Harold and Hugo were out of her grasp, but Beryl and I were still reachable. She wondered whether we were getting enough to eat. Neither of us could cook, nor cared too much about food, so she made sure that we would have at least a couple of decent meals a week. To this end, she sent us a plump roast chicken. Every Friday. It would arrive at Paddington at six o'clock. In the old days, it was Harold who was put under the charge of the guard. Now it was a roast chicken, and every Friday I would take myself to Paddington to collect what Mom considered our survival kit.

It was an ordinary Friday. Just like any other. I was woken by my Chaconne alarm. As usual we'd run out of shillings for the hot water geyser so I had to make do with a cold wash. And as usual, we'd run out of milk, so I drank black coffee then rushed to school. Classes all morning, a mercifully school-provided lunch, then Drama to finish off the week. A regular Friday. But looking back, that Friday was a day that would turn my life around.

I had time to kill before going to Paddington so I idled

about in the Swiss Cottage Café. The café's not there any more, it's been replaced by a pub, but in my day it was a real coffee house, and probably the first of its kind. There was no food on offer. The coffee was cheap and you could sit there as long as you liked. People started their novels there, or their poems, or simply exchanged gossip. The only person in the café at the time was the poet Dannie Abse, a Cardiffian like myself but far more Welsh than I. Like me, Dannie was Jewish, and found that was enough to be getting on with. But his Jewishness was strictly secondary, or perhaps didn't figure at all. Dannie asked me if I would do him a favour. He had arranged to meet a friend in the café, but he had to go somewhere for a while. Would I ask him to wait? He'd be back in half-an-hour.

'What's his name?' I asked. 'What's he look like?'

'Rudi,' Danny said. 'Not bad-looking. You'll like him,' he said. Then he was gone.

'If I'm still here,' I shouted after him.

I waited for as long as I could. Chickens ought not to be kept waiting. I rose. As I was making for the door, he arrived.

'Rudi?' I asked.

'How d'you know my name?'

'Dannie told me. He had to go somewhere. He said you should wait for him.'

'You going?' he asked.

'Yes. I have to go to Paddington to meet a chicken.'

He suppressed a smile. Perhaps I was a nutter. There were always a few of them around the café.

'You coming back?' he asked.

'Depends on the chicken,' I said.

Then I left and thought about him. And all the way to Paddington, I couldn't get him out of my head. He was wearing a grey flannel tailored suit. Suits were rare in the Swiss Cottage Café for it indicated that he was in serious employment. His face was striking. A very strong jaw, high cheekbones and liquid blue eyes. He had a Slav look about him, though with a name like Rudi he was more likely German. And probably Jewish. I was always curious about people, what they did and where they came from. I asked questions, and then I listened. I expected and often gained immediate satisfaction. But with Rudi I was prepared to wait. I would ask no questions. I wanted him to remain a mystery. At least for a while.

I was late and the chicken was waiting for me. I collected it and thought of Mom as I always did at that collection moment, and with affection. I recalled the loving that had idled between us in the fauna and flora of the farm, those moments of her motiveless caring. I saw her seasoning the chicken and placing it in the oven, occasionally basting it, then leaving it to cool when it was cooked. Then Pop, the packer, would parcel it and take it to the station. A homesick-making moment. But I had supper to look forward to, and a Friday night chicken gathering of friends, grateful for a proper meal. It crossed my mind to invite Rudi, but I thought it a bit too pushy and I didn't know how he would fit into our circle. I got off the tube at Swiss Cottage, my usual stop, and crossing the road I passed the café. I saw him sitting there, writing and alone. I went inside.

'Dannie not come yet?' I asked.

'No,' he said. 'Did the chicken?'

I held out the parcel. 'Come for supper,' I said, without thinking.

'You sure?'

'Why not?' I gave him the address. 'About eight,' I said.

I left quickly before either of us could change our minds, and on my way I bought some vegetables. Once home, I telephoned Mom as we did every Friday night to acknowledge the chicken, and to tell her that we were both well and enjoying ourselves, whether we were or not.

'Guess what?' she said. 'Celia's engaged.'

It was a loaded piece of news. Its subtext was obvious. When will that happen to either of you?

'Well I pity her husband,' I said. 'I hope that at least he tidies his drawers.'

There were usually about eight of us, and they came with what offerings they could afford. An apple, an orange, a bar of chocolate, paper cups, hoping perhaps for a beverage of some kind – for there was the occasional bottle of cider. But that night it was wine. A moselle. Donated by Rudi. What with the grey suit, and now with the bottle of wine, I had the impression that Rudi was a young man of means, but as it turned out the grey flannel was his only suit and he had nicked the bottle from his father's cellars in the city. He was as poor as the rest of us. He said little to me that evening. He spent most of it in conversation with Beryl, the subject of which Beryl reported to me when they had all gone home. His father was a wine shipper, Rudi had told her, and an amateur violinist. He had been a close friend of Paul Hindemith and sometimes he had played quartets with Friedrich Buxbaum who had been the lead cellist in the Vienna Philharmonic. Buxbaum was a legendary name among musicians. Beryl was mightily impressed.

'Get to know him a bit more,' she told me. 'I'd like to meet his father.'

'But what about Rudi?' I asked. I needed Beryl's opinion.

'He doesn't give too much of himself,' she said.

Well, that suited me. I was prepared to bide my time.

But at our next accidental meeting at the café – though I had dropped in there every day in the hope of finding him – it required only one question to enable him to unfold much of his story.

'Where were you born?' I asked.

'In Frankfurt,' he said.

Then with little prompting from me, he outlined his history. He came from a family with a long-standing wine-shipping business, specialising in hocks and moselles and exporting them to the great houses of England. In early 1938, the Gestapo had come for his father. He was not at home at the time but he got the message and fled to London, together with Rudi's sister, Madi. Settling in England presented few difficulties for his father. After perching initially in a flat overlooking Hyde Park, he bought a fairly grand home in Purley and joined the Conservative party. Even as late as 1938, he had been astonished and grossly insulted that the Gestapo had fingered him. He was a good German, and possibly more German than the Germans themselves. All that anti-

Semitism, he said, was the fault of the '*Ostjuden*', those who migrated from the east, with their beards and ringlets and long coats and sable hats. Those so-obvious Jews from Russia and thereabouts.

'My people,' I whispered to Rudi.

He smiled. 'My mother thought the same,' Rudi went on. 'I didn't know her very well. I spent most of my time below stairs with the cook and the maids, and on Sundays I was taken into the drawing room in a velvet suit to meet her guests. At night, when I was in bed, my mother would kiss me as she left for the opera, and I smelt her perfume and saw the train of her dress. I didn't really know her at all. It didn't surprise me when later on I learned that she knew nothing about opera, except what to wear for *Tristan* and what not to wear for *Rosenkavalier*. But when my father was gone I was stuck with her. She was totally helpless. She didn't even know how to pay a bill and she still thought the Gestapo would leave her alone. But then I was sent home from school. So were the Jewish teachers. My best friend, Heinz, lived a few doors away from me in Mozartstrasse, and one day I saw him taken off with his whole family Then, at last, my mother began to panic. She had a lawyer friend, not a Jew – my parents avoided Jewish company – Strauss his name was. He started to make inquiries. We could get out, he said, if we paid the blood tax, and in return we could take some of our possessions. Then he told my mother not to contact him any more. So it was up to me.'

'How old were you then?' I asked.

'Fourteen,' he said. 'I had to do everything. Get hold of

the money, do the packing. And my mother just watched me. She still couldn't believe it. We got out, finally. Nobody saw us off at the station. Not a single so-called friend.'

He smiled again and I thought I'd give him a break.

'Why d'you wear a suit?' I asked.

'Have to,' he said. 'I teach in a posh crammer in Notting Hill.'

'Your English is perfect,' I said.

'It wasn't when I arrived. I had lessons and I got into St Paul's. I'll never forget my first day, there was a concert, the school quartet. They played a Haydn. I'd never heard it before. The second movement was my old national anthem, "Deutschland Deutschland Über Alles". I left the hall. I thought it was a personal insult.' He smiled again. 'Then I went to Reading University,' he went on, 'to read agriculture, but God knows why. I dropped out after a year and now I'm teaching.'

'What's your next move?' I asked.

'My father is nagging me to go into the business. But it's not for me. I want to write,' he said. 'Poems. And I've started on a novel.'

It was at that moment that I toyed with the idea of getting him to marry me. We were so different from each other; his background, his ambition, his language and the cultural divide, all so different from my own. It struck me that a marriage based on such total incompatibility could possibly work. At least it would be unpredictable. We made no arrangement to meet again. We knew that the café would draw us both. We met frequently and, armed with his wine offering, he shared our chicken every Friday.

One evening there was a new face in the café. It belonged to Peter Zadek. He was to make a name for himself as one of Germany's foremost stage directors. But in those days he was finding his way. And he knew exactly where he was going. To the very top.

'I'm doing a production of Oscar Wilde's *Salome*,' he announced. 'Rudolf Steiner theatre.'

It was hardly the West End, and its name rang dubious education bells, but we wished him luck and told him that we would all come to the first night. We didn't see him for a couple of weeks, but at his next appearance he seemed distraught.

'I've lost my Salome,' he said. 'She refuses to do the dance.'

He looked at me, staring, and I quickly turned to Rudi in desperate and mindless conversation. I felt a tap on my shoulder.

'You look exactly right,' he said. 'I'm offering you the part.'

His offer was so preposterous that, without hesitation, I accepted.

'You're mad,' Rudi whispered.

In his way, he was right, but in my way, there was nothing wrong in being mad.

'Rehearsal tomorrow. My place. Eight o'clock,' Peter said.

He wrote down his address on an old envelope which he handed to me, and then he was gone, and I was a star with my name in lights. I couldn't take my decision very seriously. Nevertheless, I turned up on time at Peter's parents' house in Golders Green.

There was to be no audition. It was enough that, according to Peter, I looked the part. He must have been desperate. There were a number of people in the living room, and I was introduced to them one by one. The first was Renee Goddard, a seasoned actress from Germany who was playing Herodias, the queen, having saddled me with the seven veils. Then there was Herod, Michael Cacayannis who was later known as the director of *Zorba* and many other films. Michael Mellinger played the page. John the Baptist, whose head would later accuse me from my platter, was played by Neville Bewley. Then came Ernst Berk, the choreographer, who took one look at me and pronounced me perfect, though he had no idea of my lack of familiarity with the *entrechat*. I didn't do too badly on the first reading. I was buoyed by my sense of the ridiculousness. I couldn't imagine that it would actually come to my treading the boards. But I learned my part quickly, and was soon able to work without the book. And still I didn't take it seriously. Until my first workout with Ernst, when I understood why Renee had opted for the queen. Ernst worked tirelessly and I was obliged to do the same. After a week of movement rehearsals we worked to the music. Seven veils to discard, and seven different *tempi* to do so. *Largo* for the first, then through *adagio*, *andante*, a teasing *andantino*, *allegro agitato* and a final frenetic *presto* into nudity. Though such was not allowed in those days

with a censor breathing down a bared neck. I was glad of
that, because Mom and Pop had booked tickets for the
first night.

Our last week of rehearsal was to take place on the
Steiner stage itself, and though I still harboured no ambi-
tions to be an actress, I wanted to do it well and then put
it behind me and never do it again. I had managed to
involve Beryl in the production. It was her job to control
the gramophone back stage and to play the appropriate
music for the dance. Rudi would have nothing to do with
it, but he came to the first night and shivered in the
stalls. Somehow or other we got through it. The applause
was thunderous, as one would expect from an audience of
parents, aunts, uncles, cousins and friends. We managed
one review, which we could well have done without for it
was scathing. My own performance was mercifully
ignored, which was a slap in the face in itself. It was poor
Peter who got most of the flak for 'a pointless production'.
But by some miracle, and word of mouth, we played to
practically full houses. It was the near nudity that brought
them in, and earned me a number of stage-door Johnnies
of dubious repute. There were bouquets and fan letters
and the *Illustrated London News* sported a full centre-page
spread of my cavortings. Cyril sent us a copy from Lahore
and reported that I was the barracks pin-up of the month.
I had fan mail from old pupils in Birmingham. It was
more than I had bargained for, and I longed for the whole
shebang to be over and done with.

But we had another week to run. We plodded on. John
the Baptist's waxed head was slowly melting on the plat-

ter. Herod's crown had lost its gold-leaf sheen, and Herodias's jewel had fallen out of her navel. All of us longed for the last performance. When it came I played my part with gusto. Until the seventh veil. This last cover-up was of blue chiffon, and was wrapped around my entire body. According to Ernst's choreography, I was to loosen one end and carefully drape it into the pit on stage left, where a stagehand would be waiting to catch the end. This he would hold while I, to *presto* accompaniment, twirled across the stage, unwrapping myself entire. But that last night the stagehand simply wasn't there. I gazed in horror at an empty pit. I had to improvise, and I cursed that bloody nagging *presto* that forced me to strip. So despite its tempo, I teased it. I went into *adagio* mode, and slowly unwrapped myself, winding one end of the chiffon round one arm, and hoping for the best. But I would have needed at least four hands to pull it off, in more senses than one. The dance ended with its performer swathed in what looked like a straitjacket which I secretly relished, as it seemed to me to be so appropriate. So ended my foray into thespian land. We all remained friends, but with little reference to the origins of our friendship.

Rudi and I had been seeing each other regularly, and always in the café. Then one night he suggested we go out to dinner.

'Where will we get the money?' I asked.

'I've had a poem accepted. Fifteen pounds. That should cover it.'

I was so pleased for him, I reached over and kissed him carefully on his cheek. 'Can I see it?' I asked.

'When it comes out,' he said.

The publication, the kiss, the invitation to dine, all marked a milestone in our relationship. And we both knew it and wondered where it would lead.

We went to Au Jardin des Gourmets, in Greek Street. Rudi's choice. His father's firm supplied them with wine. He'd given his name when booking, hoping perhaps for favoured treatment. It was my first proper date. I was tempted to share the news with Mom, as a sort of riposte to her Celia threat. But it was too early to uncross one's fingers. I wore my best dress for the occasion. Or rather my better dress for I had only two. It was red, with a scooped neckline, three quarter sleeves, and a flared skirt, nipped at the waist with a buckled belt. I wore a pair of red wedge-heeled court shoes that Beryl had brought from India. And I combed my hair.

We met at the café. Rudi wore his usual grey suit and I thought we made a very smart couple. Despite Rudi's father's connection, we were not given special treatment. The meal cost ten pounds, and Rudi added a substantial tip. On the way to Victoria, where Rudi had to take his train to Purley, we passed a group of buskers in Leicester Square. The Happy Wanderers they were called, and they danced and sang to a drum that doubled as bells and beat. Years later they would be the subject of my first documentary film, and looking back it seemed a timely introduction. I was fascinated with them. Rudi had to drag me away. He told me a few weeks later that when he watched me watching those buskers with such pleasure, in that moment he decided to marry me. But he didn't ask me. I got in first.

'Why don't we get married?' I asked him the following week.

'Why not?' he said.

Such was our proposal, and I think we both suspected that our decision was faintly irrational. But we went ahead. I had to be presented to his parents, and Rudi to mine. I did not relish a visit to Purley. I knew that, at least in view of my '*Ostjuden*' origins, I would not be welcome. And I was not mistaken. By that time, Rudi had left home and was holed up in a bed-sit in Belsize. We were invited to Sunday lunch. Rudi hinted that I should wear a dress and stockings. I drew a line at his suggestion of gloves. I gave in on the stockings, even though it was high August, but I wore a low-cut Hungarian blouse with a gypsy skirt. Take it or leave it, I thought. I did not expect much of a welcome from his parents, but I hoped to make some headway with Madi, his sister. It was she who opened the Purley door. She was older than Rudi, and they were not close. She greeted her brother with cold formality. Rudi introduced me but Madi made no acknowledgement. She simply turned her back and led us through the hallway. I was delighted that she was ugly. Like her mother, as it turned out, and equally as cold.

Rudi's parents were sitting in the drawing room. His mother was knitting and barely raised her eyes to acknowledge me. His father at least said 'Hello', but made no mention of being pleased to meet me. I noticed, though, that he was looking down my blouse. Rudi and I had barely sat down when his mother announced that lunch was ready. She was clearly anxious to get it over and done with, to do her reluctant duty and to see the back of us. We moved into the dining room. My place was word-lessly pointed out, next to Rudi, and opposite Madi who warmed to me no more than I to her. There was soup to start with. Sorrel, Rudi told me.

'Is the sorrel from the garden?' he asked.

I knew he didn't care whether the sorrel was from the garden or a builders' yard. He was just trying to make conversation.

'The garden,' his mother replied, and left it at that.

Rudi tried once more, and I knew it was going to be his last shot. 'Bernice's family are all musicians,' he said.

He might as well have told them they were plumbers for all the interest that was shown. Thereafter there was silence. I saw no point in opening my mouth at all and under my breath I muttered that old swear-word mantra from my childhood, now much augmented, and it afforded some relief. After the desert, Rudi rose from the table.

'Thanks for lunch,' he said, and he took my hand.

I was aware that his mouth was choc-a-bloc full of curses and once out on the street, he released them. I laughed.

'I think I went down very well,' I said.

Then he laughed too, and we travelled back to London, cemented by his family's opposition.

Our next move was Cardiff. I was not nervous of taking Rudi home. Mom regarded me rather as Grandma had regarded her. As far as marriage was concerned, with despair. She knew it would take more than tidying my drawers or combing my hair for me to drop off the shelf. She would welcome Rudi with the same gratitude with which Grandma had welcomed Pop. And she did.

Rudi's charm was not manufactured; it was innate. Mom was impressed. Pop too, but with a hint of caution.

'You're both so different from each other,' he said to me when we were alone. 'What do you have in common?'

'Incompatibility,' I said. 'It's exciting.'

'You must arrange for us to meet Rudi's parents,' he said.

I knew that such a meeting would be inevitable, and in view of my acquaintance with the Nassauers, I wished it could have been avoided. We talked a little about the wedding. Cyril was due back in England so a date was fixed for after his arrival. Mom insisted on a proper wedding, a white one with bridesmaids, and in the orthodox synagogue. There would be a reception afterwards, and dancing. I looked forward to all of that but I remember wondering why we had to have a wedding to justify it. Yes, I had doubts, and no doubt Rudi did too. But we all went ahead with the arrangements. My hijacked aunts in Boston went to Filene's Basement and bought me a white satin wedding dress. The whole shebang. Train, veil and headdress. Mom booked the reception hall and the synagogue. My forthcoming nuptials were the talk of the town. And Cyril came home. And laughed.

It was with some difficulty that Rudi managed to arrange a meeting with his parents and mine. They were reluctant, but finally settled on a Sunday tea. Mom and Pop came up to London. Occasionally they would come up for a weekend and stay at the Regent Palace Hotel. We looked forward to those visits, Beryl and I, because we could take a bath for nothing. Bed-sit baths were so costly, and there were rarely enough shillings to put in the meter. So we would go to the hotel and get our parents' money's worth. Bed-sit-Rudi took advantage of it too, and both of us, together with Mom and Pop, descended squeaky-clean on Purley.

Madi showed us into the drawing room without a smile. Rudi's mother was sitting in her usual chair and, as usual, she was knitting. For the whole afternoon she sat there, and never once put her knitting down. Except occasionally to raise her cup of tea. Rudi's father was more polite. He sat us down and instructed Madi to pour the tea. There were sandwiches too, and cakes and paper doilies and linen serviettes.

'They're both too young,' were the first words of Rudi's father.

'We think so too,' Pop said. 'But they are determined.'

'What will they live on?' Mrs Nassauer said. 'Your daughter has no money.'

I noted that I didn't merit a name.

'I've begged him to join me in the business,' Rudi's father said. 'It's been in my family for over two hundred years. But no. He wants to write. Writing can be your hobby, I keep telling him.'

Pop didn't argue, and Mom asked Mrs Nassauer what she was knitting. Not that she cared, but she was anxious to keep dialogue flowing.

'It's a cardigan,' she said, and offered no more.

'Did you make this cake?' Mom tried again.

'Knit two, purl one,' was Mrs Nassauer's answer.

I wanted to leave, and so, I think, did Rudi. These people are not fit to wipe my parents' boots, I thought, and I wanted them away from such humiliation.

It was a short tea party. Rudi's father did not let up on his objections, but he was at least polite. He asked no personal questions of my parents. He was simply not curious. The teapot was empty and enough cake had been consumed. It was Pop who rose first.

'I'm glad we met,' he said holding out his hand. Rudi's father took it and smiled.

'I hope we'll meet again,' Mom said, though it was the last thing she wanted. Even then, on our way out, Rudi's mother did not rise from her chair. But she did speak.

'We shall not be coming to the wedding,' she said.

'I hope you will change your minds,' Pop said.

He was sad. But Mom was furious. On the pavement outside the house, Rudi said,

'I'm sorry. I'm terribly sorry. You didn't deserve such treatment.'

Then Mom smiled. 'We're going to have a wonderful wedding anyway,' she said.

But Pop would not accept their refusal. He wrote to them, begging them to give their son their blessing. His letter was ignored. He wrote again. Then a wedding invitation was sent and at the last minute, in icy reply, they agreed to attend.

There was the question of a dowry. It is the custom

among Jewish families to provide a daughter with a dowry on the occasion of her wedding. Over the years Mom and Pop had saved some money with this eventuality in mind. They came to London and went house hunting. They found a house on Steele's Road, midway between Chalk Farm and Belsize Park. It was a four storey Victorian house, with the upper floors rented to protected tenants for the designated rent of five pounds a week. That encumbrance sharply reduced the price. But what reduced it even further was the short lease. All of eighteen years. Pop was an old-time believer in the Labour party and he was confident that soon enough they would scrap the leasehold laws and declare all land freehold. So, with a knockdown price that was well within my dowry budget, 21 Steele's Road, registered in my name, was to become the marital home.

I was married on the 29th December 1947 in the Windsor Place synagogue, much to the annoyance of the one on Cathedral Road. It was a beautiful service, full of pomp and ceremony. The cantor sang a Hebrew version of 'Plaisir d'Amour', interrupted occasionally by the creaking of a loose floorboard in the platform on which we stood. As was the custom, Rudi smashed the glass under his foot and a cry of '*Mazeltov*' rang through the synagogue. Rudi and I kissed each other, and wondered what we were doing there.

At the reception, I watched Rudi's parents and sister. They seemed to be enjoying themselves and I had hopes for a brighter in-law future. His parents actually kissed us both as we left for our honeymoon. Not a real one. Just one of convenience. Mom, Beryl and Grandma were sailing to New York on the Queen Elizabeth. They would leave a couple of days after the wedding. Rudi and I booked a hotel in Bournemouth so that we could be near Southampton to see them off.

In those couple of days of honeymoon, we faced each other fairly and squarely. We no longer needed excuses for our union. We had done what we had set out to do, and now we had to deal with it. I'd been given a dowry, we'd been legally joined, and we had at least twenty-five lampshades and God knows how many tea sets to prove it. We didn't have to justify anything to anybody. Except to ourselves. There was only one thing to do. We had to fall in love. And we did, easily, for the seeds of it had always been sown. We were anxious to get back to London. We went to Southampton and stayed on the pier until the Queen Elizabeth sailed out of sight. Then we hurried back to our new home. And to all those tablecloths, pots and pans, sheets and blankets, presents meant to oil the precarious wheels of marriage.

'What are we going to do with it all?' I said.

'We'll keep it for our children,' Rudi said. 'Their dowry.'

It was a promise of some kind of permanence, and it thrilled me. And I was to believe in that promise long after it was clearly unfulfillable.

PART FOUR

Now comes the difficult bit, where questions arise as to the purpose of a memoir. And there's the rub. That word. Purpose. I know from experience that if one writes a novel with purpose in mind, any kind of purpose, it will be a bad novel. One writes only for oneself, and if what one writes enriches other people's lives, in any way, that is a side-effect bonus. Like a novel, a memoir should not be motivated by purpose. But purpose is only one of the traps. There are others. The greatest of these is not charity. It is therapy, the most seductive snare of all. I am a life-long, devoted, card-carrying anti-psychotherapist. I see no point in a life without stress, without anxiety, those two great sources of creative energy. In my mind, such a life would be sterile. I accept that therapy might well serve some people, but in my memoir, and it is mine after all and nobody else's, therapy must find no rationale. But

I confess that pitfall is often hard to avoid. Like now, at this moment, when I'm about to write about my marriage. That's why this is the difficult bit. Do I use this episode to vent my spleen, to assuage my hurt, to mourn my own stupidity? If the shadow and smell of therapy lurks behind a sentence, should I lay aside my pen? Then I say to myself, 'For God's sake, hold your tongue and let me love.'

Because there *were* happy and loving years. The first four or five of them. They included a belated honeymoon. Rudi wanted to show me Frankfurt, the house in Beethovenstrasse where he was born, his kindergarten, and the school that threw him out. He wanted to show me the houses of his friends and teachers, those who were never seen again. I think he wanted that journey as much for himself as for me. By way of a memorial. I remember wondering whether he was ready for such a return.

We flew to Frankfurt and arrived at the customs hall where we encountered our first German official. And that's where the trouble started. Not that we had anything to declare, it's just that Rudi resented being asked. He stared at the custom official and I noticed the vein on his forehead swelling with rage. And without any preliminaries, the Dr Jekyll who was my gentle husband became in an instant, Mr Hyde. But of course there were preliminaries. They had been nurtured in silent fury ever since *Kristallnacht*, fed daily by his father's absence, his mother's cold dependence and his disappeared friends. Nourishment enough. And he simply blew. Vitriol poured from his mouth. His early teenage German, too unripe for

ornament, without metaphor or simile, just loud and out-
spoken, laced with what sounded like my childhood
swear-word mantra, bespattered the poor customs official
who had done nothing but ask Rudi if he'd had anything
to declare. 'I'm obeying my orders,' he said, so Rudi told
me later. And I understand his outburst and applauded it.
'Obeying orders' was a phrase that was the oft-repeated
overture to six million deaths. The man, well practised,
knew it by heart, and in Rudi's view he had used it in less
innocent locations than a customs hall. I managed to drag
Rudi away. I dreaded the hiring of a car. Another official
who was given the same treatment as the customs officer.
I began to fear for Rudi's health.

We drove out of the airport. Rudi was silent and
seething. On our way we scratched several cars and I
feared for our safety. He knew his way around the city,
but he showed no interest in its landmarks. At last we
reached Beethovenstrasse and slowed down outside a large
apartment block. But Rudi didn't stop the car.

'There it is,' he said. 'Eleventh floor.' Then he did a
swift U-turn.

'Where are we going?' I asked.

'Out of here,' he said. 'As quickly as we can.'

We drove back to the airport. The vein on Rudi's fore-
head was still swollen. We dumped the car and caught the
next available plane out of the country. Its destination was
Milan. As soon as we were airborne Rudi took my hand.
I noticed that the vein was subsiding, as he cried out the
Mr Hyde in him. I held him close, without need of words.

Rudi had a cousin in Milan. His father's sister's

daughter. Her name was Marguerite. She and Rudi had been playmates as children. Her father, a picture restorer, had smelt danger in 1936 and he and his family had left Frankfurt and settled in Milan. Marguerite had married, an Italian Count of sorts. Rudi was keen to see her again. We wanted to tour a little, so we arranged to meet her in the Milan cathedral. We watched her as she entered the nave. She dipped her fingers into the font and, crossing herself, she knelt before the altar. My stomach turned over and I had to sit down in the nearest pew.

'What in God's name is she doing?' I asked Rudi.

'She married a Catholic', he said. 'And she converted.'

I was no less intolerant in those days than I am today. I will suffer fools, but not traitors, for that is how I viewed Rudi's cousin. I couldn't understand how she could have turned her back on her roots, and on those disappeared children she must have played with as a child, and joined a sect whose very head had collaborated so freely, who had sent thousands of her people to their deaths, who had happily facilitated the escape of those who had taken them. I could barely shake her hand as she greeted me. This is not a good honeymoon, I thought to myself. I think Rudi too was disillusioned and we spent little time with her and all in whispered German in the cathedral. I watched her leave, and with the same charade.

'D'you happen to have any pleasant relations?' I asked Rudi.

'Yes,' he said. 'In Israel.'

I was relieved that his stock was not wholly sour.

He suggested we go to the church of Santa Maria delle

Grazie to see da Vinci's masterpiece. Why not, I thought. I'd already had a quick course of betrayal and it seemed apt to round it off with *The Last Supper*. It's a shock to see the painting in the flesh, as it were, having been reared on its picture postcard. Many years later, I saw Picasso's *Guernica* at the Prado and I had the same feeling of disbelief. The postcards of both had been so real, that there had been no thought of any source. I stared at *The Last Supper*, and had to force myself to credit its originality.

We had arranged to spend the last week of our honeymoon on Lake Maggiore. It was an idyllic time. Rudi spent much of it working on his novel *The Hooligan*, while I lazed by the lakeside reading *Anna Karenina* for the first time. That lake sojourn seemed to me to be our proper honeymoon. I think that Sharon, our firstborn, was conceived at that lake. When she arrived Rudi seemed disappointed. He'd wanted a boy. And when Rebecca was born, almost two years later, he thought I was doing it on purpose. I didn't try again. By then I was beginning to be afraid of him.

We needed to move to a larger house. Despite its short lease, we managed to sell Steele's Road and, again with the help of my parents, we moved to number 10 Compayne Gardens. My extended dowry, and still in my name. It was a beautiful house of three storeys. The top floor was a ready-made self-contained flat which we were able to rent out. By this time, Rudi had joined his father's business. Reluctantly. But there were compensations, his secretary being one of them. Her name was Anne. She often volunteered to babysit for us. I thought her pleasant and obliging. It took me a little time to realise that she was pleasant and obliging in areas that had nothing to do with babysitting. But even then I refused to believe it. I simply couldn't afford to give it credence. But I drew the line at babysitting. It was a feeble rebuke, but that spinelessness was to be the colour of all my subsequent protests. Looking back now I marvel at my crass stupidity. And laugh a little.

Every time Rudi sowed a fresh oat I was given a present. A blouse, a skirt, a dress. Over the years, I acquired a wardrobe of Rudi's conscience. Then, for a while, there were no gifts, and I hoped that all oats had been sown. But it was the mere lull before the storm. One day, out of the blue and for no reason at all, Rudi gave me a beautiful necklace. I knew I was in for the big one.

Her name was K. She was ugly, thick and sublimely boring, or so I had to think when I saw her, seething as I was with jealousy and rage. But later, when the fury had subsided and I had found my own happiness, I still found her boring beyond belief. I couldn't imagine what Rudi saw in her. I noted that she had a boy bum. Perhaps that was a clue. She was an accessoriser. She worked for a fashion house, and her job was to choose bags, belts, scarves etc. to go with the apparel. She herself was an accessory, though not decorative, and certainly of no vital importance. Poor K. I pity her now. For thirteen years Rudi promised to marry her. And never did. 'Give me time,' he told her. He said the same to me when I voiced a feeble protest. And for thirteen years I gave him time, so monumental was my stupidity.

It was during this time that a Mr Elias Canetti came into our lives, and seemed to lodge there permanently. I disliked him from the start. I thought him a scrounger, but Rudi was much taken with him. Mr Canetti had written one novel, *Auto Da Fe*, which Rudi had read and was deeply impressed by. According to its author so was the whole of Europe. Over the years I got to know this man and I realised he had but one single talent. That of self-promotion. He created mystery about himself. If you wanted to phone him, for instance, you had to let it ring twice. Then you had to put the phone down and ring again. Certain people could approach him, but only if they'd had a reliable recommendation. I thought it all rather pathetic. My father met him once and declared him evil. And as it turned out, he was right, though evil might have been an overstatement. He did not have the imagination to be evil. He was wicked rather, depraved, vicious and spiteful. His own life was dull and uneventful, and to compensate he would create intrigue in the lives of other people.

My marital situation fascinated Canetti, and he curried favour with K in order to stir the pot. He moved around Hampstead couples and loners doling out destructive advice and waiting, with infinite pleasure, for the shit to hit the fan. He himself was married to a rather gentle victim, Vesa. He told me once how he envied me my children and what a sorrow it was for him that Vesa couldn't have any. Later I was to hear from Vesa herself that it was he who did not want any children and insisted on taking steps to prevent it. I hated that man. He was the only person in my life that I have ever hated. And I loved that hatred. It inspired me. It was almost a creative force. One day, I was driving up Haverstock Hill and Mr Canetti, deep in filthy thought, crossed the road in front of me. It was not a pedestrian crossing, and I could, quite legally, have killed him on the spot. 'He came out of nowhere, m'Lud. It was impossible to pull up.' But I refrained. I needed him around so that I could go on hating him. About thirty years later, he left England and went to live in Zurich. Nobody regretted his departure. As he had so often predicted, and had no doubt promoted, he won the Nobel prize and eventually died of old age. I marvelled that a man of such perverse nature could die of natural causes.

But now there was another death. And far more mourned. Pop. My father. He was sixty-eight years old and too young to die. In November 1956 his heart, which had troubled him for many years, finally let him down. I remember his first heart attack. One summer, we were playing on the beach in Porthcawl. Pop had gone into the water. He was a fine swimmer, but the water was very cold. From the shoreline and our sandcastles, we viewed his difficulties and heard his call for help. He was rescued immediately and placed on a stretcher. I remember that despite his pain he managed to say thank you to those who carried him. I was angry when Mom phoned to tell us he'd died. 'But I didn't even get to know him,' I shouted at her. And it was true. I knew *about* him. I knew of his

wisdom, of his caring, his humour and his eternal gratitude. But they were only the facts of him. I had not yet
related them to his flesh.

His funeral was fulsomely attended. Pop had been
much loved, and the community turned out to pay its
respects. The hearse made a detour on its way to the
cemetery in order to pass the newly built synagogue in
Cyncoed, where Pop used to worship. And as the hearse
approached, a great blaze of lights draped the temple and
faded as the cortège passed by. I sat in the car with
Grandma and held her hand. She was crying piteously,
ashamed that she had outlived him. When it was all over,
I began to miss him terribly. I dedicated my first novel to
his memory and it was then, after the words were out,
words of him and for him, that I taught myself to know
him.

Back in London, the 'give me time' scenario droned
monotonously along. It was now in its sixth sterile year. I
had begun writing, and that pursuit kept me calm.

I had also started making documentary films. In those
days you couldn't work in film unless you were a member
of the union and you couldn't join the union unless you
were working in film. So I began as a film cleaner, hoping
to acquire a technician's ticket and later on effect a transfer. I worked at Colour Film Laboratories off Baker
Street, starting at seven every morning. For the whole
day, I would clean negative from spool to spool. I ran my
carbon tetrachloride cloth over the pictures, and I got
high on the smell. I stuck it out for two months, then I

worked as an assistant editor, and later on sound. A friend, Derrick Knight, who ran his own documentary film unit, gave me my first chance as director. The film was about a child with celebral palsy. Thereafter I made films on various subjects, mainly dealing with children. I loved the work, and between film and novel writing I kept my sanity; helped by my friendship with David Mercer.

David was a playwright who had rented the flat on our top floor. At the time, David's wife Dilys had left him, and no doubt for good reason, for David was an over-emotional philanderer. He was one of the finest playwrights of the time – of his plays, those that featured on The Wednesday Play slot are memorable. At the time, his frenetic affair with novelist Penelope Mortimer had come to an end and he was not in the happiest of humours. Neither was I. Most evenings, we drowned our sorrows together, David in beer and myself in vodka. I am not by nature a drinker. Vodka looks like water so it made me feel less sinful, and I was grateful for its numbing effect. But David was a serious tippler, and often at night he would come home somewhat the worse for wear. His bedroom was on the second floor, whereas ours was on the first, directly on the landing. More often than not, he couldn't make the second floor and he would flop down on our bed, boots and all, and sleep off his hangover. Rudi didn't seem to mind, and David didn't mind whether Rudi was there or not. Our bed was his occasional crash pad. No questions asked.

At the time, David was working on a film script, and he had many visitors. Among them another tippler, Zbyszek

Cybulski, a Polish actor of some renown. A Polish James
Dean. He had starred in Wajda's *Ashes and Diamonds*, a
role that had jettisoned him into international fame. He
stayed with David for a while, and David must have told
him about his crash pad, for whenever he found it necessary. One time when Rudi was away travelling on
business, I'd gone to bed early and was asleep when I was
woken by a movement by my side. I assumed that it was
David and I turned to sleep again. But I felt bare feet on
my own. No boots. In any case, David never slipped
under the covers. Whatever or whosoever was there, was
bootless. And blanketed. A murmur of passionate Polish
then purled my ear; and I was glad that Rudi was away.

From time to time, we went en famille to Purley. Though
his parents seemed uninterested in our children, Rudi felt
a connection should be maintained. I went under duress,
seeing it solely as a duty. His parents' attitude towards me
still reeked of disapproval, but at least Rudi's father had
mellowed somewhat. Although they quarrelled daily, he
was satisfied that Rudi had joined the business. But Rudi's
mother remained distant and cold.

Mrs Nassauer kept chickens in a tidy section of her
posh Purley garden, and as we were leaving that day she
presented Rudi with a carton of half-a-dozen new-laid
eggs. We were standing on the linoed floor of the kitchen.
'That will be three and sixpence,' his mother said. I
laughed, but I saw Rudi's forehead vein swelling. He said
nothing. He simply opened the carton and dropped the lot
on the floor. I don't know whether you have ever tried

mopping up a fresh egg. Leave alone six of them. They're like mercury. Untrappable. I stifled a giggle as I envisaged Madi on her oh-so-virtuous knees chasing the yolks and albumen along the lino, and it warmed the cockles of my heart. We left them to it, and I never went there again. It was one of the few times that Rudi and I felt united, though it was on account of such a trivial matter. I still had hopes that soon he would stop asking me to give him time.

Not long after that visit, Rudi's father fell ill. A cancer of the tongue was diagnosed. A horrible affliction, and Rudi was deeply depressed. It was a condition difficult to witness, yet Rudi alone monopolised visiting hours, for his mother and sister preferred to think he would recover. When, after a painful and mercifully short struggle, his father died, Rudi was left with the maintenance of the business. He took in a semi-partner, a get-rich-quick wide boy who knew nothing about wines, but was a friend and a good companion. They had much in common, he and Rudi . . .

Alas, it was the dying season. Sometimes, when Auntie Annie or Mom were away, I would go down to Cardiff and stay with Grandma. It was a big house and she feared being alone so I shared her bedroom. It was a large room, with space enough for two double beds, a heavy Victoria wardrobe, a dressing table and a tallboy. When Grandma was ready to go to bed, she insisted on my retirement at the same time. And she told me that she didn't mind if I watched her undress. I sat on the second bed, a witness, though there was nothing to see. Even so, her movements in themselves were a spectacle of sorts.

First, she donned her nightdress, and over that a tent-like garment that tied at the neck so that any undressing procedure was invisible. She placed her hands underneath the tent and began to manoeuvre. I surmised she was unlacing her corset, for the movement was accompanied by a series of sighs and finally with a large gasp of relief. She was smiling. She extracted the garment and laid it full out on the bed. It was whale-boned and frayed with long service. She smoothed it with her hand in what seemed like a gesture of gratitude. Then she went sub-tent again, fumbling. In time, she withdrew a skirt, and afterwards a half petticoat. These she folded neatly and laid them on the corset. A breast-binder came next, followed by a cardigan. These two were laid on the corset. Then she loosened the tent straps and stepped out of her covering. She was now dressed for bed. But before retiring, she rolled her clothes into the corset, tying the laces, and she lay the little parcel at the foot of the bed. I was convinced that if no one had been in the room, if she had been entirely alone, she would have followed the same routine, and I wondered whether ever in her long life, she had dared to look at her body.

Dear Auntie Annie, her life-long carer, brought her morning tea to her bed. Grandma could not be woken. She had died in her sleep in her ninety-seventh year. The rolled-up corset lay, as always, on the foot of the bed, as though if called upon it would be handy for a second coming.

My Auntie Annie began her own slow fade. Her caring

role had ceased, and she missed a long-ago love that she had lost. When she eventually died, seven years later, the doctor put two and two together, and called it cancer.

Auntie Annie was the first of my mother's siblings to die, and it was her death, rather than my Grandma's, that threatened her sisters and brothers with their own mortality. But they were let off the hook for a while, and given time to cope with their grief and their fear. I knew that I was next-but-one in line, but I have to confess that the notion of mortality had rarely bothered me. All my writing life I have harboured a sneaking assurance that God, or whoever is in charge of these things, would not take me mid-sentence. An arrogant assumption no doubt, but that is perhaps why I am afraid to stop writing. When you sneeze, they say the devil has free entry into your soul, so 'Bless you' is said to send the evil spirit on his way. It's like showing the Cross to a vampire. So in my rare idle non-writing moments, I often say 'Bless you' to myself, then quickly write a word or two, to prove I'll not be caught napping.

I rarely asked about the affairs of the business. Rudi talked to me in terms of turnover, which sounded prosperous enough, and I was happy to let him get on with it. Yet there appeared to be an underlying element of anxiety about him. I knew that something had changed and that the something was probably related to K. Onc night we went out to dinner, and returning home we parked the car outside our house. It was our habit to stay in the car for a while to chat, and I took the opportunity to ask what was troubling him. I was not prepared for his response. He offered no preamble. He knew I would not buy excuses or rationale.

'K's had a baby,' he said. 'My baby.'

I took the information into my mind. Nowhere else. As long as it was only in my mind, I could deal with it. I had to shield my body from total breakdown. I knew that there was one question that had to be asked. One that was as vital as the enquiry as to whether or not there is a God. Well there is. And He's not good.

'Boy or girl?' I asked.

'Boy,' he said.

Then my mind could cope no longer. My body protested, and with some relief, I opened the car door and threw up on the kerbstone. I managed to stagger into the house and a night of non-sleep. I didn't tell my children, they learned the facts from eavesdropping. Later on they told me how they resented my silence and couldn't understand why I didn't throw Rudi out of the house once and for all. I should have talked to them. I should have listened to them. They had the wisdom of children which, to my cost, I did not respect. I knew that the phrase 'give me time' was no longer viable. I knew that a baby was a fact. That a baby grows. That it does not go away. K lived but a quarter of a mile from our house, and my greatest fear was to run into her and the son that I had failed to give to Rudi.

'Get them out of here,' I told him. 'Or I shall kill them both.' And I meant it.

He took me seriously and said he would find them a

place on the other side of London. But for that he needed
money. We had only one source of capital, and that was
my dowry. In those days it was almost impossible for a
woman to acquire a mortgage, so he suggested that I
transfer the house into his name in order to raise a loan.
I was anxious to get her out of my sight. It seemed, even
to me, a very high price to pay. But despite the sordid
treatment that I had undergone over the years I didn't
want Rudi to think badly of me. I was the sort of person
who gets deeply on my own nerves. I agreed to his suggestion. The title deed of my dowry was transferred into
Rudi's name, and K was moved to Holland Park. A year
later, Rudi went bankrupt, and since he was personally
responsible we lost everything. My once-dowry, now in
his name, became the property of the receivers.

We had only a little money saved and nowhere to live.
Now would have been the time to cut my losses, to leave
Rudi and start afresh. But forgive me, dear reader, if you
are still with me, I was sorry for him and so I stuck
around. By that time, I had made a number of documentary films, mainly about handicapped children and adults.
One of them, *Stress*, about parents of handicapped children, had picked up a few prizes. It was seen by Dennis
Mitchell who, together with Norman Swallow, was head
of Documentary at Granada at the time. He offered me a
three-month contract. My salary enabled us to pay the key
money on a flat in Hampstead with a reasonably controlled
rent, and so we moved yet again. It was a beautiful flat on
the top floor, with a great view of sunsets over London. In
the beginning, however, I spent little time in it. I was in

Manchester while Rudi was son-hopping and clearing his debts. I was entitled to a lift in the Granada Monday jet to Manchester, returning on the Friday. It left from Northolt airstrip. On my first journey out, there was only one other passenger on the plane. He sat in front, and as I entered, he asked, 'D'you work for me?'

'Who are you?' I asked.

'Sydney Bernstein,' he said. 'I own Granada.'

I trembled. 'Yes', I admitted, and gave him my name, then I shrank into a seat far behind him.

It was a silent ride. At the airport he escorted me to a small car, which he told me was mine for the length of the contract. I drove off a little way, then stopped in a lay-by and contemplated my good fortune. I would tell Rudi, I thought. But then perhaps I wouldn't. No. But I would tell my girls. And suddenly, although I'd been away from home only a few hours, I missed them.

I made just one film for Granada. It was called *Dear Mum and Dad*, and it was about Broome House, a home for children in care. I was not too happy with the film. Children in care are by nature suspicious, and wary of strangers. I was not long enough in their company to win their trust, and the result was a film that had little depth. Once the rough-cut stage of the film had been reached we were obliged to show it to the then Head of Programmes. At the time it was Dennis Foreman, since knighted. I was terrified. He chose to sit next to me in the viewing room, which did little to steady my nerves. About halfway through the film I felt his leg rubbing against mine; a pushing rather, and an insistent one. I was appalled. I thought it gross. Such an action in such a place and at such a time was deplorable. I ached for the film to be over. When the end came and the lights went up he turned to me, smiled and said, 'Well done'. In view of his behaviour he could hardly have said otherwise. As he left the room, I noticed that he was limping. And rather badly.

'What's the matter with his leg?' I asked my editor.

'It's a wooden one,' he said.

I wanted to rush to him and beg his forgiveness for my unwarranted thoughts, but he was gone and to another viewing. I ran into him occasionally during the rest of my stay in Manchester. He would return my smile politely but he clearly had no idea who I was.

I was glad to get back to London. I was glad to be with my girls. Rudi was rarely at home since he had returned to the wine business. He was good at his job and an excellent buyer. He knew his wines. That knowledge was in his blood. He was doing well and it seemed that soon enough he would be discharged from his bankruptcy. But I had lost interest. My film career was moving on. Derrick Knight, who had first employed me, was approached by UNDP to make films on UN projects in the Third World. They had chosen Africa, South America and Indonesia as their targets. I was given Indonesia. There were three areas in which the UN had mounted projects. Education, agriculture and women's welfare. It was a heavy assignment and it both frightened and excited me. We were a small crew, four of us in all. Two on camera, one on sound and myself. I was to pick up an interpreter in Djakarta, but first I was to go out alone. I was to spend two weeks researching and scriptwriting together with all the production work. I flew to Djakarta.

On arrival at the airport, and passing through customs, I was aware of a great change. I couldn't account for it, and it was not until I was driven into the city, and had met those who had been delegated to look after me, that I realised the nature of the change. I am but five-foot-one-and-a-half-inches tall. I have had occasional neck problems due to conversations held standing with people taller than myself. But in Indonesia, I was practically a giant. I was astonished at how a simple matter of height can radically change the quality of conversation. Whereas hitherto I had obeyed, now I could order. I tried not to take advantage of my new-found imbalance, though occasionally, when dealing with bureaucratic officials, I found it came in handy.

I spent a couple of days in the capital, my first acquaintance with the developing world. Djakarta, like most third world capitals is pockmarked with monuments, rude fingers aimed at the sky. An obelisk here, a column there. Occasionally the monument honours a national hero, but in the ranks of patriotic devotion, the turnover is pretty rapid. Very often the hero has fallen from grace, and possibly from the gallows too, before his monument has been unveiled. And to cover this contingency, columns erected to honour human beings tend to be very high so that the features are quite unrecognisable, except from a helicopter. When necessary, the only item to be changed on the stone edifice is the legend, easily replaced by the name, rank and credits of the current favourite.

The branches of the UN umbrella, those dealing with infrastructure, education, agriculture and health, were housed in the main street of the capital, almost next door to each other. Yet no branch knew what the other was up to, or seemed even to care. During my six weeks' stay on the island, I saw ample proof of this non-cooperation. I found newly built polyclinics with no means of access, modern libraries with few books, prestige laboratories without skilled teachers. In hospitals I found doctors too intent on the study of heart transplant to bother mastering the treatment of their doorstep diseases of bilharzia and yaws. In the villages, farmers were issued with bales of fertiliser and pesticide, but they remained unused and gnawed by rats. Instructions for their use were written in German. In the fields, the tractors rotted away for want of maintenance skill. Overall it was a depressing picture. Depressing too, because the films were being sponsored by the UN itself, and such sponsorship would limit honesty.

It was suggested that I travel to Djogjakarta in Central Java where there were many UN projects in operation. I was provided with Wan, an assistant and interpreter, and together we took the Djakarta–Surabaya express. I think that after all my questionings and stated doubts, the authorities in Djakarta were glad to see the back of me.

I had been booked into the Ambarrukmo Palace Hotel, but I had no intention of staying there. One cannot make films from hotel rooms. I asked to be lodged in a village close to the people and projects I would write about. Wan took me to the nearby village of Harbobingangun and lodged me in the house of Roschak, the medicine man.

Then he scuttled back to Djakarta and left me without language. Now I am much of a verbal person, perhaps too much so, but I had to learn new ways of making myself understood. Roschak and his family helped with sign language and slowly we learned about each other.

The central room of the house was reserved as sleeping accommodation. A long rush-covered bench was set against one wall. On it, Roschak and his wife, Trees, slept side by side, together with their six children placed in order of age. Guests were settled at the very end of the bench, and it was there that I spent many peaceful nights. Every morning Roschak held his clinic in the clearing that surrounded his house. He would treat each patient differently. Sometimes he applied herbs to various parts of the body, or finger massaged, or rubbed on herbal lotions. Other times he would simply talk to them and offer no other treatment than that. Thus the morning passed and the glade slowly cleared. But one morning it seemed that the whole village had gathered in the clearing, together with those who had travelled in betchaks from neighbouring villages. The glade was full of men, women and children, and all of them seemed in a state of high excitement. I had no idea of what was happening and I wished that Wan were around. Shortly, I heard the distant sound of a gamelan band. I looked down the path that led to Roschak's house, and indeed there was a troupe of players seated on the back of a lorry that was inching its way towards the clearing. In the centre of the group there was a throne-like structure on which a young man sat, garlanded with flowers and clearly someone of great importance.

The truck pulled up at the clearing and four village men hoisted the throne on to their shoulders, bore it across the glade and settled it under a tree. The band stopped playing and for a while there was silence. Then Roschak motioned a woman in the crowd to approach the throne. She knelt humbly before the man and talked to him. The man listened and then he whispered to her, smiling most of the time. After a while she returned to her place and seemed satisfied. Roschak then urged another woman to go forward and the routine was repeated, and so on throughout the whole day until everybody had somehow or another been seen to. Then, as daylight fell, the man was carried away to the accompaniment of the band and the cheering of the crowd. I had no idea of what had taken place and I had to wait until Wan came up from Djakarta to explain it to me.

It seemed that the village housed a man whom we in the West would diagnose as schizophrenic. Once or twice a year, or possibly three times in a good year, he would endure an episode or, as Roschak said, he would enter one of his turns. It was in such a turning that the man was possessed of divine wisdom, which was why villagers approached him with their problems and he would advise them.

'What kind of problems?' I asked.

'Mainly domestic,' Roschak said. 'Their marriages, their children. Or sometimes about their crops or their health.'

'D'you believe his advice is reliable?' I asked.

'Without doubt,' Roschak said. 'His condition is God-given. His thoughts are of a divine dimension.'

I then asked Roschak about his own work, and what he talks about to his patients.

'I ask them about their dreams,' he said. 'I tell them what they mean and how they should act upon them.'

'Does the name Freud mean anything to you?' I asked.

'Freud.' Roschak thought for a while. Then, 'Does he live in Djakarta?' he asked.

By the time the film crew arrived, I was pretty confused about which world was 'developed', and which world was called the 'Third'. I was disillusioned too about the effects of UN aid projects. The notion of 'them' and 'us' prevailed, that the 'us' is right and the 'them' backward. In the name of Coca-Cola and hamburgers their culture and inheritance were slowly being eroded. I found it hard to promote birth control to women with large families since having a large family was part of their cultural tradition. They knew that if they had ten children only half of them stood a chance of survival, but their attitude to death was culturally different. You can't in all sincerity tell a woman who is reared on ancestral worship to go on the Pill. There's no point in telling them that there's a world shortage of food, while the rice is rotting in the go-downs waiting for the market price to rise.

'It's not our many children,' one farmer's wife told me. She was a protest leader of sorts. She had heard about the burning of coffee in Brazil, and the butter mountains. She knew we buried apples and tomatoes in England. 'It's not our many children,' she said again. 'There's enough food in the world for everybody. It's just your rotten capitalistic system.' And I had to agree with her.

We spent our last night in Djogja at the Hindu temple of Prambanam, witnessing the enacting of the Ramayana, and I wondered how much, if anything, we in the West had to teach them.

I was homesick. I missed Sharon and Rebecca, but I was not ready to return. I feared for the state of my marriage. I knew that a decision had to be taken and I rather wished that Rudi would take it and thus shoulder the consequences. Tom Cowan, an Australian who was the cameraman on the film, and a good friend, wanted to visit friends in India and he suggested I come with him. So we took our time coming home. We stayed with some film-maker friends in Madras, then moved on to Calcutta and Nepal. We were unashamed tourists. New Delhi and Agra were our last ports of call, then back to London and whatever chaos awaited.

It was a quiet chaos, with underground rumblings. A dog would have sensed the earthquake and run for cover. But we had no dog. The girls told me that Rudi had hardly been at home during my absence. I didn't have to wonder where he had been. On my first evening home, I unpacked and distributed the presents. Sharon and Rebecca were very happy with their batiks, their silks and sarongs and their farmer's jackets. I kept Rudi's present till last. It was a black silk smoking jacket with a pale pink silk lining. I had bought it in a Delhi market, and as the man had wrapped it, I was suddenly drenched with a hope that all would be well again. I handed it over. Rudi unwrapped it silently and slowly, as if loath to discover its content. When he had laid it bare, he hung it out. He said nothing. He didn't even try it on. He simply re-folded it and put it aside. 'Thank you?' I asked. He shrugged. He felt too guilty even to acknowledge it.

A few days later he had arranged to take the girls to visit his sister. Madi had entered an arranged marriage with a millionaire who manufactured paint. They lived in what estate agents call a 'des res' in Deanshanger. I had been there once, reluctantly, and had been given a tour of the house. Everything was in order as if it had never been touched. The bathrooms housed white towels folded in anal obsession to within a half inch of their linen lives, and unused bars of white soaps were arranged in hair-raising symmetry. There was a room that they called the study. The desk was bare but for a line of sharpened pencils lying to attention without a point out of true. Books lined the shelves, all bound in green Florentine leather. I suspected that they were mere spines. Next came the master bedroom. It was ornate in the extreme. Silk curtains draped the windows, silk lampshades bracketed the bed, a silk counterpane was covered with silk cushions, all geometrically placed. The room was so busy with décor that it seemed to me that very little went on in the bed. Then on to other rooms with the same deodorised asepsis. Madi followed me around the tour with an ashtray in her hand. I never went there again.

Sharon and Rebecca were none too keen on the visit but they agreed for the sake of peace. Rudi had wanted them to dress up, with stockings and the like, but they were not prepared to go that far. A row ensued. Rudi naturally blamed me for their intransigence and he hit out, striking me on the head. Sharon thrust herself between us and gave him a bit of his own medicine. It was the last straw. 'I'm leaving,' he said. 'I want a divorce.' And he was gone. I heard one of the girls say 'Good riddance'. Then they went to their rooms, thinking perhaps that I wanted to be alone. I sat down. It was that one parting word that rang in my ear, that thundered and echoed and thundered again. Divorce.

I thought of all the turbulent years we had spent together. I thought of all he had taught me, of his guidance into areas that to me were hitherto unknown. The literature, the music, the food, the wines. But despite the Camembert, the Proust, the Spätlese and Trockenbeerenauslese, despite the Rilke and *Der Rosenkavalier*, I was still a nice Jewish girl from the provinces, and to my parochial ear, the word 'divorce' was rude. Very rude. It could well have been added to my childhood swear-word lexicon. I was shattered. When the phone rang, I hoped it might be Rudi with a change of mind. But it was an old friend inviting us to dinner the following Saturday.

'I'm on my own,' I said. 'Rudi's left.' Saying it aloud didn't help. I still couldn't believe it.

She hesitated. 'Oh,' she said, and she sounded very cross.

I had disturbed her boy, girl, boy, girl dinner placements, and that wouldn't do at all.

'I'll ring you,' she said and she put down the phone.

Sharon and Rebecca were very supportive. Both had boyfriends and their own lives. I felt that they wanted no debate, so I stressed that in no way were they to blame. I knew that I had to deal with it on my own. What nagged me most was my sense of total unwantability, and I was determined to prove that this was not so. The search for such proof is not commendable, but I was not concerned with ethics. All I wanted was proof, and I had little care how I sought it. So I went on a rampage of coital punishment. I don't remember the names or the faces, they didn't matter. In any case, there was no pleasure in it. Two weeks of such self-destruction provided proof enough, and I was calm once more.

After Rudi had left, I received a series of gentleman callers. They had come to give solace, they said. But few men do solace. Solace is a woman's domain. I was grateful that they came, but gratitude was my sole response. Most of them got the message and did not call again. Except for one, for whom the penny never seemed to drop. I shall call him Paul Short for discretion's sake. Paul sent flowers and phoned almost every day, long after solace was required. I was sick to death of his concern, so every time the phone rang I would yell, 'If that's Paul Short, I'm out'. Sharon and Rebecca would often say it for me, and one of them would answer the phone and declare my absence. 'If that's Paul Short, I'm out', was my automatic and reflex response to every ring of the phone. One afternoon the phone rang. My daughters were washing their hair, and I was bound to answer. No prizes for guessing. I was caught by Short. I felt badly about him and I thought that since the girls were going to be at home, I might as well invite him to supper. I sniffed his gratitude through the wire. 'Eight o'clock,' I said.

He arrived as the clock struck. His face was concealed by his bunch of roses and the blooms trembled from his bated breath. I knew I'd made a terrible mistake, but I made him welcome. We conversed politely during a pre-prandial drink. My girls were silent and I blessed them for not giggling. The first and second courses passed peacefully enough, and I no longer regretted having issued the invitation. Until the dessert. I had made chocolate pots, and as I was serving them around the table the phone rang, and I, like some robotic Pavlovian dog, screamed my automatic response. 'If that's Paul Short, I'm out'. My treacherous daughters fled from the table to answer the phone, as if it required four hands to lift the receiver. They did not return, and I was left with the echo, mockingly irretrievable, of my gross blunder. I realised that there was only one course open to me. And that was to tell poor Paul the truth. I spelt it out as gently as I could. He took it badly. He rose from the table without a word. Then he crossed to the coffee table where I had arranged his flowers, and in one movement he yanked them out of the vase, indifferent to their thorns, clutched them with what was left of his pride and left the flat. I was grateful that he had taken them. His gesture was the least that I deserved.

My landlord lived in the ground floor flat and called regularly to collect the rent. One day, he asked me if I would be interested in buying my flat. As a statutory tenant, I was entitled to buy at a price well below its market value. I told him I would think about it. It only made sense if I were to buy and then sell, and thus make a profit to enable me to settle elsewhere. The flat would not be difficult to sell. And I had not been happy there. I had to accept that my married days were over and done with and that I needed to start afresh. My mother thought it a good idea, and she lent me the money for the purchase. I had recently won the Booker, and sold a couple of films, and all that helped too. So I became a property owner once more. Then I had to make the decision of when to move. I had been told that moving was a traumatic experience, one that involved decluttering and dispossession. But I was faintly seduced by both. I wanted to start out clean. So I toured the flat searching for a positive reason to up sticks. I found it in the kitchen. My cooker. It had done me good service in its time and had collected much crud in so doing. Its appearance disgusted me, and I asked myself, 'Shall I clean the cooker or shall I move?' No contest. Moving, however traumatic, has got to be easier.

So I put the flat on the market and I hid when people came to see it. I was ashamed. Not only of the crud on the cooker but of the dust on the skirting boards, the gritty grouting on the bathroom tiles, and the ring of limescale in the loo. I was ashamed too of all the coloured soaps the estate agent had persuaded me to put in the bathrooms, and those silly bowls of pot-pourri. I cringed when I thought of them. The agent also suggested I make proper coffee and time its filtering to coincide with the doorbell ring of a punter. The aroma of coffee, he said, was a selling point. They came and went, the flat hunters. One of them, Mr Whitbread, was hooked. He'd never seen a more exciting apartment, he told me, and he couldn't wait to move in. I began to resent him and I wondered why I was moving out.

I started to pack, keeping dispossession in mind. My wardrobe came first. I wondered why, with only one bottom, I needed seven pairs of trousers. I folded the surplus and put them in the bin-liner for Oxfam. The sweaters, the suits, the dresses, all the stuff I was hanging on to in case I lost weight. But I hadn't and probably never would. So more and more piled into bin-liners. I took a break then. I was postponing the most difficult part of the exercise. A true baptism by fire. The books. Yes, the books. If you want to find authentic superfluity, take a look at your bookshelves, for there it overspills, loud and clear. I'd read most of them though I remembered only a few, and I was forced to conclude that my library, in the main, was mere wallpaper. It's hard to discard books, especially if you're a writer. I had to decide which volumes to keep.

Most of my friends are writers, and their books would remain. I decided that I would scan each title and ask myself the question, Can I read this book again? Can it bear rediscovery? And on the basis of that criterion, I was appalled at the avalanche of discard, and the sudden nakedness of my many shelves. I scanned what was left. The nineteenth century English and Russian classics, and much of contemporary American fiction. Poetry, some plays, Shakespeare and the Bible and all my school books. My greatest achievement was the ditching of that whole

Bloomsbury fraud, together with Proust. I'd managed the first four books with little pleasure and I swore every New Year to finish the cycle. And each New Year, I felt guilty. So it was a relief to be rid of them. But I kept the bronze statue of the Booker lady. My girls had given her underarm and pubic hair, so that she looked more human. I was ready to move. I decided that I liked the process. Moving is an enriching experience, and because of that I do it quite often. But at the time, I settled for a lovely flat in Greencroft Gardens, in my lost-dowry land, and the past had indeed become another country.

But Rudi still hovered. He was constantly in touch and he asked if he could see my new flat. I invited him over. He said that I had hung the pictures incorrectly, and that this piece of sculpture should be here and not there. Nuisance as I might have been to him, he couldn't quite dismiss me altogether. When he had left the marriage, he had not gone straight to K. He had hovered a while. He was wise enough to know that the play that we had enacted together for so many years, that 'give me time' drama, was essentially a three hander, and that the moment one player was dropped from the cast, the play wouldn't work any more. And it didn't. But he finally succumbed and went to live with K and Adam, his son. And faced the consequences. I invited Adam over from time to time. He was an innocent and I had no quarrel with him. He looked very much like Rudi, he duplicated all his features. Except for the ensemble. That he took from his mother.

As time passed Rudi still rang me often and occasionally

we would meet. I was always glad to see him, but I worried about his health. He was putting on weight, and seemed not to be caring for himself. He was gambling a lot at casinos, that time honoured sex-substitute pursuit. One night, he asked me out to dinner. We went to an Italian restaurant in Soho. He did not look well, and he seemed depressed. He was silent during the hors d'oeuvre and I noticed that he was eating with little appetite. When the entrée was served, he stared at his plate and out of the blue he launched into an attack on K. I listened with a certain pleasure.

'She's so unutterably boring,' he said.

'Well she has to have a talent for *something*,' I muttered.

I was tempted to say that he'd made his bed and he could bloody well lie on it. But clearly it wasn't on her bed that he was lying.

'I can't bear to touch her,' he went on. 'She doesn't read, she doesn't listen to music, she has no conversation. She thinks that Shostakovich is a toothpaste. And those big glasses she wears – she says it's the fashion. That's all she seems to care about. Fashion. She's a nothing, I'm afraid.' He put his hand on mine. 'God help me,' he said. But he managed a laugh. I noticed that he was not eating. 'I don't feel too well,' he admitted. He laid his hand on his chest. Rudi had beautiful hands and I was saddened by his gesture.

'Shall I drive you to the doctor?' I asked.

'No. I'll feel better tomorrow,' he replied.

But he didn't. Very early the next morning, he phoned me.

'I'm in Harley Street,' he said. 'The doctor is taking me to Hammersmith hospital. Will you come?'

I was afraid to ask him what had happened. I suspected a heart attack and my own heart fractured a little. I didn't want to lose him. I felt that between us there was too much unfinished business. It was still too early to ring my girls. I would do that from the hospital. I made myself ready to leave. But I was nervous. I had seen K only once, and that was years ago. I was a coward, so I took Harold with me for protection. But at the hospital there was no sign of her. Evidently she hadn't been informed.

Rudi was in intensive care. It was a mild heart attack, the doctor told me, and he was responding well. We went into the ward. Rudi's chest was bare but dotted with pads connected to a machine. He looked far better than he had in the restaurant. He even managed a smile. I took his hand. There was an identity strap on his wrist. His name and his address. I knew the name well enough. It was the address that puzzled me. For it was mine. He noticed my bewilderment. 'Oh, it's all so confusing,' he whispered. I kissed him and wished him a speedy recovery.

I didn't visit again, but my girls went daily and reported back. He was mending. He would be discharged in ten days, but then he would have to convalesce and be cared for. I'll say this for K. Boring and stupid as she was, she cared for him well, and he made a full recovery. After a while, he left her. I heard that she was suffering greatly, but I couldn't be bothered to pity her. I just wondered whether she took off those hideous glasses to cry.

My old Lothario had once again fallen in love. Fit and

hale, he was coming up for more. He bought himself a flat in Hampstead and set himself a-wooing. P was a very different kettle of fish. At the time she was slowly making a name for herself as a painter. I liked her for she had done me no harm. She was pretty and talented. And certainly not boring. She did not think that Shostakovich was a toothpaste. I wished them well of each other.

Or did I?

Left to right: Me, Harold, Beryl, Cyril (sitting)

Me as Vanity Bag

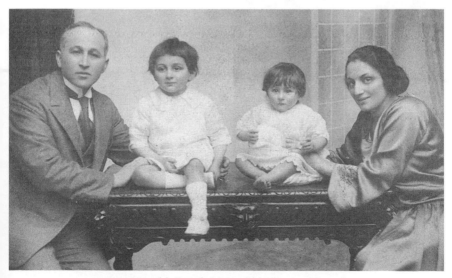

Pop, Harold, Beryl, Mom (pregnant with me)

Roath Park Girls' School.
Me, middle row, fourth from left

Harold at the piano

Harold,
Mom,
Me, Cyril, Beryl

Left to right: Mrs Nassauer, Mr Nassauer, Me, Rudi, Mom, Pop, Grandma (Millie)
at our wedding

All Seven Veils adorn Salome when she starts to dance before King Herod. Each flimsy cover symbolizes varying moods

First Veil, which is white, expresses purity and is worn over head. It is discarded to the tempo of slow and appealing music

AFTER SCHOOL HOURS

PHOTOGRAPHED BY PETER WAUGH   DESCRIBED BY ISOBEL ROBERTSON

The Lord Chamberlain lifts the ban on *Salome*, the play with Dance of Seven Veils, and London sees it for the first time

CHALK in hand, twenty-three years old Bernice Rubens demonstrates on the blackboard the oddities of French grammar. Four hours later the scene changes. The blackboard, the desks, the schoolchildren are no more, but Bernice still holds the stage. She is taking the part of the dancing Salome in Oscar Wilde's play of the same name.

Clad in shimmering veils, which she discards one by one, she dances before the throne of Herod. The background music, first slow, then carelessly light and gay, gradually quickens in tempo, portraying anger, intensity and passion, ... overpowering crescendo sounds to the wild beating of drums. With that comes Salome's final abandonment as she casts off the seventh veil.

Oscar Wilde's version of the Biblical story was written originally in French fifty-six years ago, and centres round the bewitching Salome, daughter of Herodias, who, at her mother's instigation, agrees to dance for Herod. In return for her dancing, he grants Salome's request for the head of the prophet, John the Baptist, but is so shocked by her exhibition that he has her killed, too.

Thought the crux of the play, the Dance of the Seven Veils, at one time thought to be too suggestive and provocative, is in reality only a very small part. Nevertheless, it was solely on account of the Seven Veils dance that *Salome* was banned from the stage by the Lord Chamberlain—a ban which lasted forty years.

Its recent revival by the Centaur Theatre Company, established to promote wider interest in drama, marks the first public performance of the play in London since the ban was lifted.

Most of the young Centaur Company engaged in this venture are

No Veil on knowledge when Bernice Rubens works from nine until four at Burgess Hill School, Hampstead. She usually teaches English, but here she is instructing class in French grammar. Bernice is working out her notice, and then she will devote all her time to stage

As Salome; me teaching, 1946

Me with short hair, 1950

Washing up, newly wed, Steeles Road

Rebecca, Me, Sharon, Rudi, 1952

Left to right: Rebecca, Carla, Beryl (Mark), Cyril, Mom, Sharon, Pop, Harold, Liza (Mike), Me, Paul

Posing for publicity photo, early 1960s

Me in India, early 1960s

Sharon and Rebecca in the kitchen

Sharon and Mom

Mom and the 6 p.m. call

Mom and Me, 1985

Cardiff – Mom's place.
Left to right: Beryl, Harold, Cyril, Me

Me and Rudi, 1993

The Booker statue, won in 1970

With 'my boys', Joshua and Dashiel, Cuba, 2001

Cuba, 2001

PART FIVE

I was pushing fifty. I had published a number of novels; I had made a number of films. Yet my waking thought each morning was What shall I do when I grow up? I have that same waking thought to this day. Such a thought must point to an area of discontent. Did I make the wrong choice? But I never *chose* to be a writer. My first book just happened. I was lucky with it. To write a second was inevitable, and thereafter I was hooked. But writing was never a conscious choice. I just got saddled with it. Shall I be a cellist when I grow up? Too late for that, but the craving nags. I play every day, but I never practise. Consequently I don't improve. I listen to Casals' Bach suites, and I am riddled with jealousy, an envy I have never felt in the face of a great novel. I am blessed to be without envy of other writers, especially my contemporaries. Envy is a bitter pill. It is never swallowed. It is chewed, and its taste is acrid. I can read Tolstoy or Melville, Austen or Dickens with never a thought that I could have been a contender. With Casals it's different, which explains the envy. So I punish myself as I listen to his recordings, but the pleasure more than outweighs.

The move to Greencroft Gardens proved to be constructive. And pleasurable. I was back with my family. Cyril lived down the road with Janet, Emily and Saul. Harold lived round the corner and my two girls and grandsons were in short driving distance. Beryl was fiddling in the pit of the Welsh National Opera but she visited London often enough. So did Mom, and she stayed with me. For the first time in many years, I felt protected by family, especially Cyril, now in the London Symphony Orchestra.

When I moved into Greencroft, one of my first inspections was the cooker and oven. Pristine, unused, gleaming. I reckoned it could withstand at least three or four novels before the accumulating crud necessitated a further move. I settled down. But not for long. I was on my travels once again. The *Observer* sent me to Basutoland, or Lesotho as it is now called. At the time, most writers and musicians honoured the boycott of South Africa and its ruthless apartheid regime. But there was no way of reaching Lesotho except by way of South Africa. I remember shutting my eyes and ears and, with some difficulty, my mouth, until I reached Maseru, the country's capital. I was to write a feature on Lesotho's women.

It is a country ruled almost entirely by women since their menfolk were away over the border working for a pittance and board, in the goldmines. I sought out four women who, in my mind, covered all aspects of government in Lesotho. Miriam was a leader of sorts, who organised women's groups and baby crèches. Rosie was a prostitute, thus contributing to the largest source of income in the country. Della was a white Catholic missionary fighting a losing battle, and Ellen was the owner of a shebeen. Between them all, I thought I might transmit the hopes, despair and occasional joy of Lesotho's women.

Miriam was my guide. She lived alone with her four children, testimony to four paid annual leaves of her gold-mining husband. She was lucky. At least her husband came straight home from the railway station and stayed by her side for his two weeks above ground. At the station, Rosie and her kind would have offered him her services as they did to the other men on leave. And many of them, their pockets bulging with accumulated wages and year-long woman hunger, were trapped by their longings, and often returned on the next train, penniless and still unsatisfied. Rosie had a special routine. Most mornings she spent at the station and in the alleys and shunting-yards around. Then she would rest a little before going to Ellen's to fortify herself for her evening's work. The shebeen would be crowded. Ellen's business boomed when the trains arrived, but she would encourage the men to go home. She herself had been the victim of one whom the Rosies had seduced. She hadn't set eyes on him for years, and no longer wanted to. Her shebeen profits sent her children to the missionary school, clothed and fed them, and even paid the occasional fine when the police, though drinking themselves, felt obliged to issue the standard penalty. Rosie drank just one glass, then went back to her hut to change. Her evening's work was the more profitable and contributed generously to the country's economy, the hub of which was the casino and the Holiday Inn Hotel alongside. Built by South Africans and with South African money, it catered for those double needs of the rich South African male. *Le rouge et le noir*. Especially *le noir*. Gambling was illegal in South Africa, and relations over the colour line strictly beyond the pale.

On my last day in Basutoland I ran into Laura, an eighteen-year-old beauty who worked as a croupier in the casino. She was with her mother, and both were dressed in traditional finery. They were obviously off to some kind of ceremony.

'It's the last pull,' Laura said to me. 'D'you want to come?'

I asked for some explanation, and when it came I politely turned down their invitation. Since birth, Laura's mother had daily pulled her labia, stretching them. As she grew the labia lengthened and today's ceremony would celebrate the final pull which would render Laura ready for service.

'How?' I asked in my ignorance.

'The labia act as a cosy sheath for man's penetration,' Laura's mother said, as Laura hid her face. 'It's for his pleasure,' she added.

The news depressed me. I had often seen Laura at the casino scooping the cards on the black-jack table and sometimes the chips on the roulette. She was an innocent and pious Catholic girl. Educated at the convent school, Della had tried to persuade her to a nun's vocation. But Laura had three brothers and a long-absent father. Her mother worked as a cleaner and had difficulty making ends meet. So Laura had to refuse the veil, and spread the chips instead. Yet with all this show of independence and courage, she still considered man as her master, one to be served and pleased even though her stretched labia added nothing to her own pleasure. I wondered how much ground the Women's Liberation Movement would have gained in Basutoland.

I drove back to Johannesburg and was stopped at Ladybrand, the border town. I didn't expect problems. I had authority from the *Observer*, after all. But the officials were not busy that day and they decided to go to town. They searched my luggage and my person. The *Observer* did not impress them – they had probably never heard of it – but they found a book in my luggage and that did for me. It was a novel called *Kinflicks* which, unknown to me, was banned in South Africa. Because of its dirty bits, I suppose it was not considered suitable reading for those God-fearing, righteous and pious white folk, god-fearing and righteous and pious enough to trample on every human right. After three hours of mindless questioning they finally let me go, and even wished me a good journey.

'But you will not be coming back,' one of them said. He had stamped my passport forbidding a return to South Africa.

'I'll come back when you lot are out,' I shouted at him.

But Mandela was still on Robben Island, and I wondered how soon I could return.

That assignment depressed me and when I returned to London I decided to give writing a rest for a while and to immerse myself in a situation that had long disturbed me.

It was happening in the Soviet Union. It was pre-Gorbachov days. There was no *perestroika*, no freedom of any kind. It was the era of *samizdat*, the self-publication of underground information through the writings of banned and persecuted writers. It was through this channel that the news filtered through of Jewish refusniks.

I had two cousins and an aunt who lived in Moscow. Pop's brother, Berl, had weathered the two wars in the capital. He had died shortly after the war and his widow and two daughters remained in the family apartment. The LSO made an annual visit to the Soviet Union and Cyril would call on them and bring back a report. They lived frugally, he told us, in a cramped apartment, sharing it with two other families. Cyril had asked them if they wanted to leave but they had protested their joy in the Soviet system, and how happy their lives were. Shortly before Cyril was to leave on another Soviet tour, we had a letter from Israel. By fair means or foul, the three of them had managed to get out, and they cursed the land they had left. 'The flat was bugged, Cyril,' they wrote. 'We could say nothing.' But they were not refusniks. Had they been, it was doubtful that they would have been allowed to leave. The refusnik situation was desperate. To leave the country, one had to apply for an exit visa. If the applicant was Jewish, it was more than likely that a visa would be refused. The applicant was then labelled a refusnik. But if he was Jewish, he had more reason than most to leave the Soviet Union at the time because of its virulent anti-Semitism. The consequences of his refusnik status were dire. He became unemployable, and if out of work for too long, he could be charged with parasitism, a crime that merited a prison sentence. If he insisted in his protest he was labelled a dissident, and dissidence in the Soviet Union was an acute sign of mental disturbance. So he would be straitjacketed into an asylum where he would be treated as a schizophrenic. It took enormous courage to apply for a visa in the first place.

At the time, I was reading a book by Alexander Herzen on the reign of Nicolas I of Russia in which I learned that those who were opposed to his regime were put into lunatic asylums. After almost two hundred years, it seemed to me that nothing had changed.

I had a good friend, Nan Greifer, who was working with the '35' group on behalf of refusniks. She was a child refugee from Poland, but apart from her mother tongue she spoke a fluent Russian. She was asked by the organisation to go to the Soviet Union to try to meet with refusniks and get an overall picture. She invited me to go with her. I was sorely tempted. I had certain root connections with the country and it was tempting to see where Tolstoy had lived and Pushkin and Dostoevsky. I doubted whether Nan would have access to any refusniks, but she was hopeful. She had built up a list of contacts. We left together on Aeroflot in May 1982. Nan warned me that there might be trouble on arrival. A year earlier she had been refused an entry visa because of her involvement with the '35' group. But that group had since acquired a much lower profile.

We arrived at Moscow's Sheremetyevo airport mid-afternoon. By the time we reached passport control I was aware that we were being followed. As we waited our turn, I saw one of our uniformed tailers staring at Nan and moving himself into a position to see her more clearly. I tried to mask his view but he was already on his phone. I warned Nan but she was not surprised. At the control desk our passports were held but we were told to collect our luggage. Our bags were thoroughly searched. Then an official approached Nan and asked her to follow him. I left the customs hall and waited.

After almost an hour, there was still no sign of Nan. I was loath to make any enquiry. I did not want to draw further attention to our situation. At last she reappeared. She looked angry, but said nothing. She put her finger on her lips motioning me to be silent. We took a cab to the Cosmos hotel and rode in silence. We registered at reception and were taken by lift to the third floor. At the end of the corridor a uniformed woman sat at a desk and noted our arrival. At the time, her kind was installed on every floor in every Soviet hotel, all with the same duties. Once in our room, Nan again put a finger to her lips and pointed out the listening bug on the ceiling. There had been no attempt to camouflage it. We unpacked in silence and left quickly, anxious to be in the open air. Once outside the hotel Nan was able to tell me about her airport grilling.

She was known, she said. She was known for her work on behalf of 'those treacherous people'. She assured them that she was no longer working for them. 'Then you are welcome as a tourist,' they replied. 'But only as a tourist.' She was told not to meet with any of 'those people' and certainly not to go into their homes.

'Wait here,' she said. 'I've got to make a phone call.' She went to a public phonebox and shortly returned. 'We'll go to Pushkin Square,' she instructed. 'Like good tourists.'

Word spread around the city's refusniks that Nan was in town, and over the next few days we met with some of them in streets and in cafés, in parks and on trains. As regular tourists, we went to the Bolshoi to a performance of *Boris Godunov*. It was sub-standard and we left at the interval, our departure being solemnly noted. As good tourists, we travelled the highly impressive Moscow metro, the Bolshoi of trains. Our next port of call was Leningrad – or St Petersburg, its less tarnished title. At the airport our driver was told to wait.

'This lot are trouble,' the receptionist said.

An official approached us. He spoke a poor English, but his message was clear. Nan had not behaved well, he said. She had met with people who were not concerned with the welfare of the State. She had gone to their houses. She had encouraged dissent. We were to be sent home. Nan denied all the accusations and pointed out the tourist sites we had enjoyed.

'You walked out of the Bolshoi,' he said.

Nan asked permission to telephone the British Embassy to make it clear that she was not leaving of her own free will.

'You can phone from International Departures,' the official responded.

He took our tickets and passports and practically pushed us into our waiting car. At the new terminal our luggage was again minutely checked. Again Nan asked for permission to telephone the Embassy and the official assured her that she could do that from the departure lounge. But in that vast hall there was no telephone. The flight for London was to leave at six o'clock. Six hours to go. We waited. We had lunch and tried to read. We had no passports and no tickets. Simply a determination not to leave without protest. At about five-thirty, an Intourist representative appeared. He handed over our passports and tickets and told us to get on the plane. We refused. Nan insisted on a letter of explanation before we would move. Out of the blue, four uniformed thugs appeared. One of them was wearing a skirt, the only indication that she might have been a woman. A fifth brought up the rear. He was propelled by an angry Alsatian. It was the dog that did it for me. I'm frightened of dogs. Even a poodle will unnerve me. Nan didn't move, and out of loyalty I clung to my seat. But I was trembling. They grabbed me first and pulled me out of the dog's range, for which I was grateful. Nan had to be dragged, shouting all the way. We were shoved through the door and into the airplane. I heard Nan yell '*Svolochi*', which she later told me means 'scum'.

I had been thrown out of two countries, each of a dia-
metrically opposed political ideology. Yet I was the same
person. Was it possible that somewhere there was a sinis-
ter equaliser?

I was ready to settle down again, and would have done so
had not a call come from the Food and Agriculture
Association in Rome. They wanted a worldwide film of
women in rural development. I was to visit Pakistan, Sri
Lanka, Ghana, Lesotho, Bolivia and Cuba. I felt at home
in the subject and the travelling was tempting. The main
drawback was that the film was to be made by Italian TV,
with their own director. I have always thought that the
roles of writer and director of a documentary film are
indivisible. I couldn't see how it could work. But I was
persuaded that this was not my problem and so I set out
once more.

I was provided with a UN passport. In many of the
countries I visited I was often approached by CIA agents.
My passport was a useful cover. I refused their sugges-
tions, of course, in spite of their offers of payment, and I
wondered how many UN officials were moonlighting.

My first port of call was Islamabad, where I was a
guest of the Bhuttos. Benazir was a little girl at the time,
and her mother held a tea party for me for the sole purpose of displaying her caskets of jewellery. I wondered
what it had to do with women in rural development. Mr
Bhutto dropped in to say hello. In hindsight, that visit was
a salient memory. So too was my visit to Bolivia when I
landed at La Paz airport eleven thousand feet above sea

level, where the air is so thin that I actually saw a fly run
before take-off. But my most vivid memory of that worldwide journey was an event in Cuba.

Carrying a UN passport is not always to one's advantage. With that document I was accepted as a guest of the
Cuban government, and as such I was given a government
official as my minder. I was to be shown only what he
thought was good for me. To this end, I was taken to a
house in an industrial area in Havana and invited inside to
see how a typical Cuban housewife lived. Señora Vilna was
fully prepared for my visit and proudly showed me around
her spring-cleaned home. The showpiece was in the
kitchen where pride of place was given to the refrigerator.
'A present from Papa Fidel,' Señora Vilna explained, and
proudly she opened its door. Its contents could well have
graced a well-heeled American's freezer. I mumbled my
appreciation of Papa Fidel's generosity. I was then hurried
out to visit another household. We drove to the bottom of
the street, and the driver turned left. I looked at my
minder who seemed to be having a seizure. '*Right* I said,'
he yelled in the driver's ear. A U-turn was impossible and
we were obliged to go round the block once more, and
thus pass Señora Vilna's house for the second time round.
Just in time, it seemed, to see two workmen lugging the
fridge down the front steps and a tearful Señora Vilna on
the threshold. I pretended not to have noticed.

Afterwards I was allowed a visit to the Lenin national
park, and to Hemingway's house, neither of which had
much to do with women in rural development. My
minder was finally persuaded to take me to meet with

Raoul, Fidel's brother, who was in charge of rural matters. He took me to a village polyclinic. I knew that both the village and the clinic had been built by the Israelis before Soviet intervention. The village closely resembled the town of Arad in Israel. When I pointed this out, it was strongly denied. Israel, in Cuba, was not flavour of any month.

I was short of any concrete material, but I managed to cobble a script from hearsay and deduction. Not the most honest piece of work, but I had little choice. At the time, the Soviet Union was Cuba's sole ally, and it struck me that both places had much in common — with their vigilantes on every street, their armed guards on every hotel floor, their dissenters in gaol, their writers imprisoned and their homosexuals living if not dying in abject fear. Before leaving the country, I went for a walk along Havana beach. The shoreline is dotted with trees. A man was lurking behind one of them, and as I passed he sprang out in front of me and exposed himself. I gathered up what was left of my Higher Certificate in Spanish and I asked him, 'And what did the revolution do for you?' He smiled and pointed to his barely erect member. It was answer enough.

Because of my UN status I was given a great send-off, but I was never more glad to leave a country behind. No more travel, I decided. When I got back to London, I found the piano out of tune and the cello A string had snapped. First things first. Then I sat at my desk and faced an empty page. The Cuban experience compounded by the recall of the Soviet journey had left a sour taste. I

knew that to lift that depression I had to write about it.
And I did, much later, in a book called *Brothers*. But at
the time I was in no writing mood. I wanted to stay at
home and be with my family.

It was about this time that Penelope Mortimer came over
for supper. I had just read the first part of her memoir,
About Time. It impressed me deeply. She had managed to
write about her parents, both unloving and often cruel, yet
despite the damage they had done her she portrayed them
with such understanding, and even with a deep affection.
Penelope was not an easy companion. She was prickly and
she didn't suffer fools, and I saw much of myself in her.
But she had boundless compassion and a lovely, biting
sense of humour. I told her how much I liked her book.
She said she was having problems with her agent.
    'Who's yours?' she asked.
    'R,' I said.
    'Are you out of your mind?'
    'Why?' I asked.
    'I was with R once. Just once,' she said.
    I should have paid attention to Penelope, but after
many disagreements, R was still my agent and continued
to be so until she herself was withdrawn. I behaved
towards her rather as I had with Rudi. I didn't leave her
because I didn't want her to think badly of me.
    R was an emotional blackmailer, and a great cocktail
hostess. With these two questionable assets she had managed to gather a group of novelists, playwrights and film
directors. Which brings me to the films. Films of two of

my novels. I didn't write the scripts of either. I wasn't asked. But that did not bother me. In truth, I was happy not to be involved. A book is a book and a film is a film. And their grammars are different. I was simply happy to have a bite, nay two bites of the cherry. And I didn't find it difficult to hand over my work to another writer. I'd written the books, and taken full responsibility for that, but the film was someone else's problem. My philosophy is to take the money and run, which in my case was not very difficult because the money was never very heavy.

The first film was an adaptation of *I Sent a Letter to My Love* in 1979. The novel was set in the little seaside town in Wales, Porthcawl, where we used to spend our summer holidays. It's the story of a brother and sister, both in their sixties, who live together but hate each other, with a hatred that lies close to the borders of love. The brother is very handsome, but he is a cripple, bound to a wheelchair. The sister, lonely and envisaging her brother's death, places a box-number advertisement in the local paper seeking a male companion with a view to marriage. She waits for what she expects will be a hundred or so replies. For weeks she waits for the post but nothing arrives. Then, one day, when she has practically given up hope, she receives a letter, a very moving letter describing the writer's loneliness. 'I have to tell you', the letter reads, 'that I am a cripple.' The letter is from her brother. At first she is very angry, but on rereading the letter she realises what a lonely and bereft life her brother leads, and she resolves to write to him under another name using the address of a poste restante. The book then largely consists of the letters between them that grow more and more intimate and erotic until, through the letters, they learn to love one another.

Nobody in England wanted to make the film. In those days the English were emulating Hollywood. The story was too downbeat, too parochial, and faintly incestuous. After a couple of lapsed options it was bought by a French company. The film was shot in Brittany on a Celtic coast resort very much like the seaside resort in Wales. It was beautifully cast. Simone Signoret played the sad spinster of the tale, and Jean Rochefort her crippled brother. Delphine Seyrig played Simone's friend. It was directed by Moshe Mizrahi, who had already directed Signoret in *Madame Rosa*. Lise Fayolle produced the film and became a friend. She invited me to Brittany to meet Signoret and to watch the filming. I was nervous. I had long been an admirer of Signoret's films and I had read her autobiography. She wrote well, and almost honestly. I looked forward to meeting her but I had no idea of what I would say. As it turned out, it was she who broke the ice.

Moshe Mizrahi met me at the airport and drove me to a health resort where Simone was staying. She met us in reception. She wore a white towelled bathrobe and some sort of turban on her head. She was drinking from a glass of what looked like milk, but was probably a disguised *pastis*. She came towards me and took my hand. She gave me no time to say anything, any of those words that I didn't know how to use, and said

'I want to play Madame Sousatzka.'

'I'd want that too,' I replied, and meant it heartily.

Madame Sousatzka was the heroine of an early book of mine, and was under option at the time. But of all that later. The ice had been broken. She took our arms and led us into an empty lounge and then she excused herself.

'I'll have to make three difficult phone calls,' she announced. 'I'll be back soon.'

When she had gone, I asked Moshe if he could find out who she was phoning. I felt that if I knew, I could identify those three problems of hers and I would learn to know her intimately. Shortly, she returned and provided the answers herself.

'Yves,' she said. (Yves Montand, her husband.) 'My daughter,' I noticed that she did not name her, 'and my mother.'

She said no more, but I felt an immediate kinship. At one time or another I too have been faced with three difficult phone calls. And the recipients were exactly the same as Simone's: Rudi, for starters, in never-ending difficult moments; one or other of my daughters during a period of prickly mother-relationship; and my dear mother, who now, though much mellowed and loving, still managed nevertheless to make me feel guilty. I felt that Simone was anxious to be left alone, possibly to mull over her phone conversations. We left, and I did not see her until a few days later when shooting began.

Film-making in France was a cottage industry. There were no studio sets, no trailers, no lavish canteens. The film was shot entirely on location, and food was eaten in local bistros with their local wines. I stayed with the crew for a whole week and marvelled at the quiet and controlled professionalism of cast and crew. Simone's every appearance, even without words, was magical. As was Jean Rochefort, who pierced his part not with any intellectual reasoning but with an innocent and innate compassion. When I left, Simone told me to come to Paris for the opening.

'We have to talk,' she said.

I assumed that she wanted to discuss the role of Madame Sousatzka.

The French are serious filmgoers, and the film entitled *Chère Inconnue* opened in eight cinemas simultaneously. At two o'clock, we folded ourselves into a little Deux Chevaux. Lise Fayolle was driving, Simone sat beside her and I was squashed in the back seat of the car with Yves Montand. As we approached the first cinema, Simone wound down her window a fraction and fixed her lizard eyes on the queue. It stretched well around the block and was slowly moving. We stopped the car and waited a while until the queue had been absorbed. Then Lise rushed to the cashier's box and returned with the news of the 'gate'. It seemed that Simone's payment included a percentage of the takings. We moved on to the next cinema, and the next, and the next, until we had covered them all, and all with the same routine. It was a novel way of touring the city. I did the round only once, but I gathered that it was a daily routine until the run was over.

I was happy with the film, happier than I have been with any other transfer of mine. I stayed in Paris for a few days, and on my last I had lunch with Simone. I had prepared a Madame Sousatzka talk, but that role was not mentioned. And I cannot mention what was. That matter, those three difficult phone calls, belong to Simone's memoir, not mine. Some problems, painful as they may be, are difficult to share. Until a stranger arrives, and in that stranger you can confide in the sure and certain knowledge that you will never see them again. There will be no follow-up phone calls, no enquiries as to one's well-being. Sitting with me at the table, Simone could empty her pain into a reliable void. Such was our exchange. I came away and wept for her. I never saw her again.

I'd had good mileage out of *I Sent a Letter*. There was the book, a film, a musical and a play. The musical opened, and mercifully quickly closed, in an off-Broadway theatre. I went to the first night. The libretto was banal in the extreme, and the music simply dreadful. I found the whole performance quite ridiculous. But it didn't worry me as it was yet another grammar for which I was not responsible. The play was different. I had written the adaptation and I alone was accountable. With the exception of one superb actress, the late Kate Reid, the play was poorly cast. But Arvin Brown was a sensitive director. The play opened in the Long Wharf Theatre in New Haven, Connecticut. Mom, Beryl, Sharon and Rebecca flew over for the first night, and they were joined by my two hijacked aunts from Boston. It played to a packed house for the whole of its run. It was no doubt a commercial success, but it was not offered a transfer to Broadway. Arvin was disappointed and admitted that it was possibly due to the casting.

But my most vivid memory of Long Wharf was not my play. It was my meeting with Quentin Crisp. He was performing his one-man show at the smaller Longwharf Theatre. We were staying in the same hotel, the Howard Johnson opposite the theatres, and we had breakfast together each morning. He was in every single particular an original. He would appear in the dining room at nine o'clock so immaculately turned out that he squeaked. I wondered at what ungodly hour he had risen to forge such perfection. His maquillage was faultless, and his attire impeccable. He loved to be admired and he gave me a silent time to view him. His eyelids were blue-shadowed, as were his eyelashes, but of a darker shade, each lash a separate tendril. His cheekbones were highlit with blushing pink, as was his cupid-bow of lips. Overall lay a patina of off-white powder. Just in case anyone blind enough thought Quentin's look a natural one, the powder confirmed that the face was not of God's doing. Neither was his hair, coiffured into a roll over his forehead and sparkling blue. He ordered a hearty breakfast – the full English, he called it – and it was not until he reached for his coffee that he was prepared to offer conversation. Or rather monologue. For I said nothing and was happy just to listen. Aphorism after aphorism was laced with his philosophy. It was a total performance and clearly impromptu, for every morning it was different. And hilarious. Though I was loath to laugh, fearing I'd interrupt his flow, and after breakfast I wanted to go back to bed from the sheer exhaustion of stifled laughter. Quentin Crisp was my happiest memory of Long Wharf. I felt privileged to have known him.

*

I had lived in Greencroft Gardens for eight years and five novels. What with all the travelling, it had been a fertile time. But once again my cooker had gathered unconquerable crud. It was time to move. I went back to my old happy hunting ground, Belsize, to Belsize Park Gardens, the loveliest Belsize of all. It's a boulevard of a street, generously punctuated with trees. Now if anything in life is serious, it's a tree. Trees have a divine authority, and in mute undeniable patronage they put you in your place. That's fine by me. Besides, they are a comfort. They assure you of season. They bud, they leaf, they flower, they shed, as reliably as 'earth ... her diurnal round'. Parking on the street is difficult. At the time I drove a filthy Mini, which was so interior littered that you had to wipe your feet on getting *out* of the car. My Mini, in a street of Saabs, Volvos and the occasional Rolls, was a refreshing eyesore, and the space left fore and aft of a Rolls, in the name of decency and decorum, is usually adequate for my Mini's audacious settling.

If you were to drive by ear, which I have found is as safe a way to drive as any other, you would know that Belsize Park Gardens is a street of musicians. And mainly of pianists. The plaintive call of the odd violin or the plea of a clarinet is as welcome as any guest, but basically it's a keyboard street. And Chopin. When I made my move I think there must have been a Chopin competition in the offing, for the nocturnes, valses and études resounded along the street in Polish homage. In my garden I can hear the practice on all sides. The players seem to have difficulty with the same passages and play them over and over again. I'm often tempted to shout 'Well done', a hangover from my pedagogue days.

Belsize Park Gardens is a street of writers as well, but whereas musicians tend to practise at the back of their houses, writers work out front. There they sit at their desks brazenly displaying their trade as shamelessly as the whores in the windows of Zeedijk, Amsterdam. My own study is at the back of the house, not because I am ashamed of my craft, but because it is a room that gives access to the garden where I weed – a great therapeutic indulgence – as well as to the living room and my cello, another therapy, a weeding of a kind.

My garden seems to be a favourite meeting place for the neighbours' cats. I've yet to discover why, for I myself am not an animal lover. I can only surmise that because my flat was last owned by a psychotherapist, the cats, with their frightening all-knowingness, have gathered to cat call and take the mickey, and are not yet aware of the change of ownership. Or perhaps they feel the same about writers. I must add that there is a very high-class breed of cat in our neighbourhood. Mainly Persian, and deeply supercilious. Occasionally they get lost and notices appear on the lamp-posts offering outrageous rewards for their return. Sometimes they are advertised as sporting a sapphire-studded collar, the reason why they were nicked in the first place. And invariably they answer to the names of Pushkin or Amadeus. That's Belsize for you.

I didn't have a cat, but I didn't have mice either. I had mouse. Just the one. It lived openly in the corner of my kitchen. I expected its family at any moment but it was

obviously the black mouse of the family, the remittance
mouse, and it was alone. It moved slowly in a diminishing
circle. I think it must have been ill. I hate mice, but out
of pity I dropped it crumbs of cheese. These it ignored,
and I was glad. I hoped it would simply die, which it did
after three or four days, in its shrivelling circle. It must
have died from sheer giddiness. I regretted not giving it a
name. Not a Belsize one. Fred would have done. At least
that's the name I gave to a kind neighbour who offered to
bury it, together with a 'Here Lies' sticker. None of
Fred's relatives came to his funeral. Poor sod. Fred was a
right loner, and I've never forgotten him.

Every year, the family somehow or other celebrates
Passover, and that year I baptised Belsize with a Seder
night. I had a long refectory table, which together with a
trestle happily sat the twenty or so members of our family.
Harold was there, the eldest of us all, with his son
Michael, Michael's wife Sharon, and their three very
young sons. Cyril too, with Janet, Saul and Emily. Beryl
came, missing her three children in America. Sharon and
Rebecca, my two lovely girls, and Joshua and Dashiel too,
my grandsons, babies then, now the men in my life. It is
the custom to invite a 'stranger' to the Seder table,
stranger in the Hebrew meaning of gentile. So Mike and
Parvin shared our table. Mike, a Catholic, and Parvin, a
Zoroastrian. Strangers indeed. Where was Mom? She
must have been visiting in America. And Rudi came. He
had asked to be invited. With his years of wandering in a
gentile landscape, he hankered after his own wilderness. I
think he missed the Jew bit.

I had kept a pretty kosher house when the girls were young, having come from one myself, and had kept all the festivals, including the fast on Yom Kippur, the Jewish day of atonement. I remember one year, a bad period when I was unemployed and desperately seeking work. That Yom Kippur I told God that I would fast if He'd see to it that I got a job. Round about lunchtime I was starving. I'd lost all appetite for atonement so I told God I was going to eat, and since I'd fasted half the time, I'd settle for a part-time job. But even that didn't come my way. Thereafter my faith was diluted, and when Pop died I no longer kept the festivals. Except for Chanukah, and Seder night.

I had cooked a traditional meal with all the symbols that feature in the Seder-night service of Exodus. The wine, bitter herbs, the parsley, the salt water, the lamb bone, the matzos, the boiled eggs, and *charoset*, a sweet paste, each with a particular meaning in relation to the Seder meal. The meal itself was soup, chicken and compote. I had Grandma in mind. Every year of my childhood, she and my Auntie Annie organised the Seder table, and as far as I was able I faltered in their footsteps. Since I was the only one at the table who could read and translate Hebrew, it fell to me to lead the service. I took a few liberties with the Haggadah, the special prayerbook for Passover, tailoring it mainly for the children. They liked to ask the four questions on why this night is different from all other nights, the answer for each one describing events in the Passover story, but they were not interested in the answers. They relished the four permitted glasses of *kiddush* wine, and especially the plagues, one drop of red wine for each. They didn't mind locusts, lice or boils, but they balked at the slaying of the first-born and thought that God had gone too far. And for some reason, though they didn't mind locusts, lice or boils, they took exception to the plague of frogs, and a chorus of 'yuks' rocked the table.

The highlight of the children's evening was the hiding of the *Afikomen*, that piece of unleavened bread hidden at the start of the service for the children to search for later, an activity to keep the children involved, and without which the service cannot conclude. A reward had to be offered for its discovery, thus the children learned their first lesson in blackmail – if not the word itself, then its practice, a useful if not moral pursuit. But there were many good lessons to be learned from the Seder service. In the Haggadah, there is written a phrase that is the very core of the thanksgiving: 'In every generation, each man must regard himself as if he himself had gone forth from Egypt.' Alas, today we need no such reminders. Pharaoh has sundry names – Stalin, Hitler, Hamas, Jihad – and dwells in many lands.

I had been asked by an American company to write a book of a film. Not exactly my cup of tea, but the money was very tempting and infinitely more than I'd ever been offered for an original novel. Even so, I was wary. So I told them I needed a villa in the sun to write it. It was such a preposterous request, I half thought it was a way of pulling out. But to my mixed surprise they agreed. It was a book called *Mother Russia*, based on a dozen or so serialised scripts, and it traced the history of Russia from Tsarist times to Stalin. I worked on it night and day, and come summer when it was finished I rented a villa in Majorca. For six hedonistic weeks we besported ourselves, friends and family. We cooked, we ate, we read, we swam, we biked, we cheated at charades. Above all, we had fun. Cyril told me he'd never been happier. He listened to music most of the day, his phones plugged into his ears, strolling the beaches and smiling.

At the end of that summer, I went to Bangor to receive an honorary D.Litt from the Prince of Wales. I asked Cyril to go with me. He was always my most loyal supporter. At the reception, he and the Prince talked music. Cyril asked the Prince whether he was still playing the cello. The Prince explained that when he was in the navy he couldn't practise as his quarters were too narrow for his bow stretch. He demonstrated with his bow arm and knocked over a glass. I watched them both laughing.

I remember Cyril as a happy person. The Rubens offspring were not good with marriage. Harold was divorced, so was Beryl, and myself, though not yet divorced, had not been very much married. Cyril and Janet were happy together, and for many years. He was the youngest of our brood, and by the time he arrived my parents had exhausted their expectations. Cyril was let off the hook, and that possibly accounted for his contented spirit.

With the sale of *Mother Russia*, I was able to take a break from writing for a while. And then another bite of the cherry came my way. R was no longer my agent. She turned to film production. She had always admired

Madame Sousatzka, and it was this book that she optioned for her first production. The book had had a long option history. It was my second novel and it had came out in the early sixties. Like most of my early novels, my paddling period, it was based on family, on my brother Harold who was a child prodigy. And his crazy London based teacher whom I called Madame Sousatzka. She seemed to me to be such a weird character that I hardly believed she existed. Yet when the film came out in America there were letters in the papers from sundry piano teachers claiming to be the original model. All false, of course; the original was long since dead. The book was optioned for a film almost immediately after publication and by a woman for whom the part must have been unconsciously written, Anna Magnani, a wonderful actress who would have played the part as to the manor born. But she couldn't raise the money. After two years the option was taken up by some-body else, who also had problems with raising money. So over twenty or so years, the option was taken up, lapsed and taken up again. It was such a regular payment that I began to look upon options as my pension, so I was rather loath finally to sell it. But I did, and then the trouble started.

R kept me informed of developments. Some film producers whom I know have confessed that they are liars. They have to be. They lie to others, but mainly they lie to themselves. It's a way of feeding their confidence. R was no exception. Meryl Streep would give her right arm to be in the picture, she told me. Robert de Niro would give his left leg. And so on and so on. I had visions of Sunset

Boulevard crawling with amputees, aching to star in *Madame Sousatzka*. R expected me to swallow all of those illusions, because she herself had to believe in them. I kept the silence of total mistrust and let her get on with it. The word 'bankable' seemed to crop up repeatedly in her one-sided conversations with me. John Schlesinger was a 'bankable' name, and he genuinely wished to direct the film without offering to donate an arm or a leg. But one name was not enough. What about the star? So the star role did the rounds of 'bankable' players and it seemed irrelevant whether they were right for the part. When all the amputees had been sorted, the role was finally offered to Geraldine Page, a wonderful actress and still 'bankable'. But then she went and died. Into her shoes stepped Shirley Maclaine, an actress whom I have always admired, but not quite my idea of Madame Sousatzka. Of course I had no say in the matter, but I couldn't help thinking, rather sadly, that we had come an awfully long way from Anna Magnani.

So we had Schlesinger and Maclaine, whose acceptances had been initially on the basis of the novel, and it was enough to get started. As yet there was no script. Again a 'bankable' name was required. R was in favour of Ruth Prawer-Jhabvala – whom I thought totally unsuitable for the subject matter. With such a choice the plot thickened and curdled, I think, because the book, which had started very modestly in a little terraced house in Wales, was now on its perilous journey to India. Not that the film was shot in India, but because through Jhabvala it acquired a distinctly alien Indian flavour. That flavour was spiced by the choice of an Indian child who played the pianist. In the book the child is Jewish, and though I accepted the fact that Jews weren't the flavour of the month, and I was happy for the boy to be of another religion, I would have preferred him to be a genuine pianist. I pointed out to R that there were Japanese, Chinese, Korean prodigies by the dozen, but that there had never been an Indian pianist since India is not a keyboard continent. But R was cunning. With Jhabvala as the writer and a young Indian star and yet another Indian to play his mother, there was a guaranteed investment from Indian Airways. This is how films are sometimes made. But as I've always said, a book is a book and a film is a different grammar.

I was pleased that John at least cast the LSO as the orchestra, and featured Cyril in the band. As to the finished film, I think that the Indian connection was a mistake. Peggy Ashcroft, who played so beautifully, thought so too. She had done her share of roles in India with *Jewel in the Crown* and *A Passage to India*. She knew and loved that country, yet she was unhappy with the film. There was something offensive about Jhabvala's portrayal of an Indian family. Her attempts at humour turned out to be faintly racist.

The film was considered for the Royal Command Performance. There were a number of films in competition, but *Madame Sousatzka* had the edge because it was a family film without violence or sex. But it had one problem. It had the word 'fuck' in it. Now we know that our British royal family does not do that sort of thing, but it was hoped that the Queen Mother would not understand the word so it was passed fit for the royal ear. I waited with the others in the royal line-up. When my turn came, I bobbed to the Queen Mother. She was shorter than me, and I was able to have a bird's eye view of her tiara. It was a generous cluster of diamonds, but what impressed me most was the Woolworths kirby grip that fixed it to her hair. For a brief moment I rather favoured the monarchy.

My payment for the book of the film was long overdue. My then agent, Mark Lucas, was pressing R for the money. Eventually I got paid. Thereafter, and with some relief, I dropped her totally. But she still figured on the margins. R is well out of my life now, and when on occasion I recall her, it is not on account of her dishonesty but of my own gross gullibility.

PART SIX

Consider the notion of whoring. When practised openly in the street, it is judged illegal and is liable to punishment. But when conducted in a library, a school, a hall or an interviewing studio, the law cannot touch you and you are even occasionally applauded. But it is whoring all the same. I refer to the writer's tour. Authors selling their goods and, on occasion, even having to give them away. Whoring breaks all the rules of commerce: it must be the only trade in which you sell your goods but you've still got them. So it is with writers.

I have tried to sell myself in sundry venues worldwide, and I have a few tales to tell. In the old days, the Arts Council was the body that arranged the tours. They baptised me in the shallow end of Leicester along with three other greenhorns, one of whom was Paul Bailey who has remained a close friend. Our opening gig took place in a

bleak community hall. There were more of us on the platform than there were in the audience. We muddled
through. The following day I was sent to a school to give
a talk to sixth-formers on the art of writing, about which
I knew nothing. The headmaster introduced me. He said
he was delighted to welcome and to honour a world
famous romantic novelist whose countless works were
translated into many languages. I wondered who in God's
name he was talking about. Until he made it clear. 'Please
welcome,' he said, 'Denise Robbins.' I let it pass. I saw no
point in denying it. In any case, I had a sneaking feeling
that Denise Robbins was dead. Again I muddled through.

For my following novel, I attended the *Yorkshire Post*
lunch in Harrogate. I was placed, as they told me, among
my readers, none of whom had ever heard of me. Angus
Wilson told me he suffered the same anonymity at the
table where he had been placed. But Edna O'Brien, the
third guest, was happily known to all the high-hatted
ladies from Harrogate who shared her table.

After lunch we settled down behind a long bench with
a pile of our books beside us. I was seated next to Edna.
It was signing and selling time and a queue began to
form. Shamelessly they filed right past me, and paused at
Edna's stand. I watched as her pile of books decreased
while my pile, fed by my own paranoia, seemed in a
vision to reach the ceiling. Edna was signing her 'best
wishes' away to buyer after buyer. I cast a glance at Angus
Wilson and he too was idly looking at the ceiling. He
seemed indifferent and happy enough. But I was restless.
The sight of Edna's diminishing stack depressed me. I

stared at it, and as I did so I noticed that her novel was exactly the same size as mine. The next time she wrote her best wishes, I filched a copy from her pile and underneath the bench I managed to transfer her book jacket to around my own novel. It was a perfect fit. Then I slipped it innocently on top of her pile. I'd noticed that she was signing the first page which was blank, just as it was in my book. A bonus. Within seconds she was inscribing it with her best wishes. It was the only copy of my book that I sold.

Though such encounters would have you believe otherwise, I published regularly. It seemed I had nothing else to do. After each publication I would go down to Bush House, the overseas service of the BBC. There I would be interviewed by the lovely, but alas late, Edward Blishen, a good and serious writer who, like me, didn't take his writing too seriously. I enjoyed those almost annual interviews. He used to tell me that as a result of our meeting I might, with luck, sell one copy of my book in Sierra Leone.

I've gone whoring in sundry places and with indifferent or enthusiastic punters. The Australian/New Zealand tour is considered a good run. On my trip in 1989 to promote *Kingdom Come*, in Melbourne I was booked for a signing in the book section of a large department store. I was late, and as I rushed through the lingerie I heard an announcement over the tannoy that I would be signing books on the fifth floor. I listened to the announcer extolling my virtues. She sounded desperate. I had half a mind to cut and run. But I soldiered on.

The tannoy lady greeted me with some relief. She told

me she had been an actress in *Prisoner Cell Block H*, which later became one of my favourite soap operas, and that she was resting. She led me to the signing table. A pile of my latest book was stacked at the end. Beside it, a hopeful pen and a glass of water. We waited. My ex-prisoner from *Cell Block H* did not let up on her promotion spiel. Clutching her microphone, she listed all my books, and all my achievements, some of which were new to me. She plodded manfully on. And she called that 'resting'. At last, a woman approached the desk. I picked up the pen in expectation. She approached me direct.

'D'you know where I can get keys cut?' she asked.

'Would you like to buy a book?' the ex-con asked.

'I've no time to read,' the key seeker said. And she was gone.

I held on to the pen, though I wanted to leave. But I didn't want to desert my ex-con, who was probably being paid by the hour. So we stuck it out, both of us, for the appointed time, during which we managed to push eight or nine copies of my oeuvre.

I had better luck in another Melbourne store. When I arrived, a small queue had already formed at the signing table. One man stood out along the line of women. When his turn came, I knew exactly what he was going to say. I'd come across such buyers before and their opening line was always the same. 'It's not for me', they would explain. 'It's for my wife. She's the reader.' The subtext was clear. 'I've got more important things to do like putting a roof over my wife's head. She can afford to sit around and read your novels.' I decided to tackle him.

'What do you do?' I asked kindly.

'I'm a dentist,' he said with some pride.

I touched his arm. 'You'd make a better dentist,' I said. 'You'd make a better *anything* if you read some wonderful fiction.'

A reading of *Madame Bovary*, I suggested, would give him a better understanding of his wife, or *Anna Karenina* a better understanding of himself. *Moby Dick* would give him courage, and *Love in the Time of Cholera* would give him food for thought of his own mortality. I smiled at him and signed the book he bought. I rather hoped he wasn't going off to a drilling appointment. God help the poor open-mouthed sod in his chair.

I fared little better in New Zealand. I was booked for a radio phone-in in Auckland. It was a late-night programme. I was interviewed by a rather tired producer, who then invited listeners to phone in with questions and comments. We waited while he struggled with words to pad the interview. The phone was dead, and went on being dead, and we had yet three-quarters of an hour to go. I began to feel very sorry for my interviewer, and after half an hour of a dead phone and his desperate padding I suggested we call it a night. His gratitude was sublime. But worse was to come the following evening.

I was to talk to a group of women readers and writers on my own work and its sources. The hall was crowded with an enthusiastic audience. I talked for over an hour and there were many intelligent questions. I was satisfied. Until, over a cup of tea at the end of the session, a woman approached me with a friendly smlle.

'I want to thank you,' she said. 'Your books have changed my life.'

I was flattered. Until she continued.

'I particularly liked the one about the . . .'

Then she went on to outline a plot that I would never have considered. Yet the story was vaguely familiar. It was the plot of my friend Beryl Bainbridge's book, *Injury Time*. I let the woman ramble on, though I was much put out. I had, after all, been speaking for over an hour about my own work. I decided not to let it pass. I looked her straight in the eye.

'I think you think I am Beryl Bainbridge,' I said.

The poor woman blanched. She looked as if she wished the floor would open up or that she could go down the drain, the wrong way down the plug hole, of course, as these things tend to operate down under. She staggered out, stooped, and I felt sorry for her.

I had been whoring down under for over a month and I needed a break, so on my way home I stopped off in Tahiti where every native woman looked as if she had posed for Gauguin. I was happy there, totally alone, without minders or interviewers. But there was one more selling trip to go, and for me, it was the most memorable.

Every year, the British Council organised a seminar introducing British writers to German academics. Its centre was in Walberberg, near Cologne, and it's a three-day event that takes place in a monastery. In 1994 I was invited to join the group. The other writers were Caryl Phillips, who would chair the meetings, Graham Swift,

Pauline Melville and the poet Kathleen Jamie. I had only once visited the country since that abrupt and enraged U-turn on my so-called honeymoon. The very word Germany stuck in my throat. And I make no apology for that. With my history and upbringing I am entitled. But I owed it to myself perhaps, to offer it another chance. So I joined the group. I thought very carefully about which part of my work I would read.

I had written a book called *Brothers*. It traced the story of four generations of Jewish brothers from Odessa, in Tsar Nicolas I's reign, through Wales and the mining valleys, then to Germany and back to the Soviet Union. In the German section I had written a short chapter on Auschwitz. I knew that the only way I could write about such a catastrophe was to itemise it. The facts, plain and simple. Any adjective, any metaphor, any simile would have diminished the horror. I knew about forgiveness and forgetting, but I wasn't sure of either. It worried me how the facts would be remembered. In time, when those facts had been repeated to the point of disbelief, the event would become fiction. It would graduate to the stuff of metaphor and symbolism. The story would be polluted by literature. Sooner or later it would be reduced to a rhyming couplet or at best a nursery rhyme, like the plague song of 'Ring a Ring o' Roses' sung down the generations by innocent children long after its provenance has been forgotten. Finally the event would become a myth. Mythology as a road to escape.

It was because of this fear, the fear that Auschwitz and its like would be forgotten, or myth-translated, that I decided to read that particular chapter at the opening session. It had been a painful piece to write and I had never risked reading it aloud. Already within the opening sentence, I regretted my choice. I was enraged, and I couldn't trust my voice. I decided to read it without expression of any kind, flat, unvarying, but that seemed to make matters worse. I plodded on. I was aware of shifting in the audience, and I heard a sob or two. I did not want to look at my listeners but I could not miss those who were leaving the hall. I sat down to a stifling silence. There was still an hour or so to go in the opening session but Caryl Phillips realised that my performance, good or bad, was a hard act to follow. He called for an interval in which he said we could all gather our thoughts.

We adjourned for coffee. Some of those in the audience thanked me profusely; others turned away. Except for one irate woman who jackbooted towards me and opined that my performance was tasteless in the extreme. I wondered what adjective she would have used for the ovens. When Graham Swift opened the afternoon session, he read a description of the Nuremberg trials. Caryl, with supreme tact, managed to hold the precarious balance.

During these self-selling talks, I shared platforms with writers from all over the world. I was excited to discover works by writers whom I had never read and whom I have since learned to admire. But at the same time, I came across writers whose works were, by any standard, unpublishable, yet for some reason had seen the light of day. It seemed to me that there are far too many novels, unimaginative works, crude, banal and utterly pedestrian. This thought was amply confirmed in the course of judging literary prizes.

I have sat on a number of book award panels, among them the Whitbread, the Orange, the John Llewellyn Rhys, the Commonwealth, and the Booker. I have done so more than willingly because I am hopeful of finding a new voice that in some way could enrich my own thinking. I have never ceased to hope, but rarely am I rewarded.

The John Llewellyn Rhys, like the Whitbread, is a difficult one since it covers both fiction and non-fiction, and choice between the best of the genres is almost impossible. I look back on the John Llewellyn Rhys prize with a certain sadness. There was a clear winner that year, 1979, a non-fiction book written by Joe Tasker and Peter Boardman two Everest climbers. They both attended the award ceremony a few weeks prior to a further Everest expedition. I struck up a friendship with them both, and wished them well. Joe wrote to me from their base camp in Nepal, saying how he looked forward to further meetings on his return. I wrote in reply but my letter was returned. He and Peter had been killed by a fall. It was a sadness that never leaves me.

The Commonwealth prize afforded the luxury of a trip to Sydney where it would be judged. In 1989 there was a clear winner, the New Zealand writer Janet Frame. Then there was the Orange prize. Founded in 1996, and generously funded, it was intended for women writers only. At its inception, there was a great deal of adverse criticism based on the argument that one was a good writer or a bad writer, and that gender was irrelevant. But the

Orange supporters claimed that women writers were considered second class as far as prizes were concerned and that, in proportion to men, they rarely made long or shortlists. Be that as it may, I supported the Orange as I would support any prize that promotes reading or the buying, borrowing or stealing of books. If there were a prize for left-handed writers, I would support it. Any gimmick that turns people on to reading is fine by me. So I was happy to be on the judging panel for the 1998 prize. There were many novels from women writers all over the English-speaking world, and though many of them were third-rate by any gender, there was a clutch of very exciting ones. Among them, a new novel by Nadine Gordimer, her first since Mandela's release and the collapse of the apartheid system. I was curious about the direction South African novelists would take once the enemy had been removed. I expected a long and bewildered silence in the absence of a subject that had for so long been their bread and butter. But it was this very absence that was the subject of Gordimer's new novel, *The House Gun*. And it was certainly a strong contender for the prize. Then, out of the blue, her publishers withdrew the novel from competition. On the writer's instructions, they said. She was not aware that her novel had been submitted to the Orange. Otherwise she would have objected. She did not approve of the principle of the Orange, and wanted no part in it. It was a disappointment. But there were other good novels on the shortlist, among them Carol Shield's *Larry's Party*, which was the eventual and deserving winner.

I enjoyed the Orange judging. The panel had included a librarian, an intelligent choice, for she was well aware of the pulse of the reading public. Our discussions were serious, and it was clear that every novel had been read with respect and the greatest of care. Not so the Booker. The one time I served on the panel, in 1986, I was the only novelist, and as such I did not expect anybody to take my judgement seriously. As it turned out, I was right. That year we gathered a very distinguished shortlist which included works by Margaret Atwood, Paul Bailey, Timothy Mo and Robertson Davies. Each of them was a deserving winner. I have always been a fan of Robertson Davies's work, and I thought *What's Bred in the Bone* was his best. His book was my favourite for the prize, an opinion shared by one other judge, Edna Healey.

On the decision day for our final choice we gathered in the afternoon at the Guildhall. One of the judges entered, threw her bag on the table and announced that she liked a book that made her laugh. By such a criterion, *Madame Bovary*, *Moby Dick*, *War and Peace*, *Bleak House* and sundry other classics would not even have made the long list, since none of them is a bellyful of laughs. I knew then that my choice had lost, and the prize went to Kingsley Amis's *The Old Devils*. Now that certainly was a book that made you laugh. You read it straight on a Monday, and forgot it on the Tuesday. It was a novel that simply didn't matter, and when set against any of the others on the shortlist it failed miserably. It was a depressing decision and it simply confirmed my opinion that the winners of the Booker, or for any literary prize for that matter, are the shortlist. After that appraisal, the winner is a random choice depending solely on the majority personal taste of the judging panel.

Consider now the festivals, invitations to which are another bonus for the published writer. Literary festivals abound. Almost every self-respecting city wants to get on the culture wagon, and each festival has its own particular flavour. Cheltenham, for example, is highly pleased with itself, having blazed the trail earlier than most. To be so mightily pleased with oneself is not an attractive trait in either an individual or a community. You wipe your feet when you take part in a Cheltenham festival, and you mind your manners. Which is probably why I've been invited only once. Swindon has an apt Swindon flavour. Straddled as it is midway between Wales and England, it doesn't quite know which way to turn. Whereas Hay-on-Wye has a distinctive Welsh leaning. It helps very much that Hay is a book town, and always has been, selling second-hand books and books of rare value. The little book shops on the High Street serve as a suitable backdrop to the festival. In its beginnings, Hay was very much a community festival. But it has changed. It has gained large and generous sponsorship, and as a result it has become a celebrity festival, more given to stars of variety and drama, to say nothing of Bill Clinton and his entourage. Thus the promotion of new and unknown writers has taken second place in its programming, which is a pity.

The Way with Words festival at Dartington and

Cumbria is just the opposite. You get what it says on the package. Words. And it's one of the best festivals in the canon. Then there's Harbourfront in Toronto. A generous festival with a guaranteed audience of many hundreds, leading one to suppose that there's little else to do in Toronto. Montreal, on the other hand, offers its citizens countless ways to besport themselves, yet its Blue Metropolis literary festival is well subscribed and truly international. It is one of the festivals that I have most enjoyed. Not to forget the festival in demure little Bath. Mention Jane Austen in Bath, and they're queuing round the block. Not so in Tokyo. And that's another story.

For some reason I am widely published in Japan, but I am certain that I am not so widely read. What the Japanese reader makes of my work I cannot imagine. For as with Jane Austen in Bath, there is no way I can compete with the Japanese equivalent. The name that puts bums on seats in Tokyo is that of Virginia Woolf – the punters practically kneel at her mention. In 1997 I was in Japan to promote my novels, and in the course of such promotion I was obliged to lecture to university students and their tutors on the state of English fiction. For a moment I wished that I were a Woolf fan, so that I could talk about her work with some enthusiasm. I recalled the ditching of Bloomsbury on my first flat move, and the freedom that the removal had engendered. I couldn't in all honesty fake admiration. I decided not to mention her name in my lectures and hoped to get away with it. And I did. Not because my audience did not note my omission. They noted it all right, but they were too polite to mention it. Japanese students are excessively polite, but one suspects that their tutors are putting a gun to their backs. This forced courtesy, the constant bowings of acknowledgement, seems to be equivalent of the American 'Have a nice day', and is equally suspect.

A trip to Japan is very expensive. But I was fortunate. I was able to travel widely across the country and at others' expense, for to have visited it under my own steam would have been financially crippling. The country is certainly worth a visit, and enjoyable too, if one can turn a blind eye to the excruciating treatment of Korean immigrants, and the debasement of women across the board. But to thread one's way through the high streets of Tokyo is equal to a visit to any of the great art galleries in the world. The window dressing is staggeringly original, and it is eerie to watch a milling Japanese crowd without a single camera between them.

At the end of the Japanese tour I went to the Philippines, a jaunt which meant switching from the first class of my Japanese publisher to British Council steerage. I was to share platforms with Liz Lochhead, the Scottish poet, whom I met for the first time and whose work I very much admire. But it was a disappointing tour. On the whole, British Council representatives abroad are fine ambassadors who have acquainted themselves with the traditions and even language of their posting, and are eager to promote the work of British artists abroad. But alas, here none of our meetings had been advertised and we addressed empty halls. Our per diem which was doled out by the office, barely covered the cost of a meagre breakfast, until I pointed out that we were being paid according to the old rate of exchange. The Philippine representative appeared to be unaware of it. It was a depressing tour. It seemed an awfully long way to go and a terrible waste of money to meet with no more than a couple of dozen readers who had heard of our readings by chance. I have travelled widely with the British Council and have always found those tours rewarding. The Philippines was an exception.

And so it was back to London and the state of that unmentionable apparatus in the kitchen. No, I said to myself. Not another move. I'll live with it. For it is not only the cruddy oven that lures me to the offices of estate agents, it is also the question of itching feet, and after all that travelling my feet needed a rest. And home and the company of family.

With two new men in my life, my grandchildren Joshua and Dashiel, my family had enlarged. They are grown now and I have watched over them since they were born. They are my life's greatest pleasure. Looking back, I confess that I was not the perfect mother. I love well, but not too wisely. Perhaps that might have been my qualification for becoming a good grannie. I have enjoyed the role and I have not feared blame, because I have burdened neither of them with expectation and they will tell you that themselves. At the time Rebecca was expecting her second child, Dashiel, I was writing *Brothers*, but I had no dedication. I was waiting to be told the gender of the baby. Rebecca phoned me just after Dashiel was born.

Then the dedication was clear: To Joshua and Dashiel. Brothers.

Joshua's birth had raised the question of circumcision. Rob, their father, is not Jewish, but he is an American of that generation of fashionably circumcised males. However, by virtue of their mother's religion, the children are Jewish. I held my breath when Joshua was born. I knew that Rebecca hated the idea of circumcision but Rob as a circumcised father might have presented her with a dilemma. I myself was repelled by the idea. I thought it a barbaric ritual and the very first infringement of children's rights. But I held my tongue. When the eighth day had passed, beyond the prescribed time for the ritual, I breathed a sigh of relief. Joshua would remain intact. And so would Dashiel when his time came. In my rare moments of belief, it is a wonder to me that after almost six thousand years of dogged male deliverance, Jewish boys are still born with stubborn foreskins. But as a wag friend pointed out, 'There is a divinity that shapes our ends, rough hew them how we will.' Later, Rebecca told me that she was worried about how I would react to her decision. We know our children very little, but we know our parents even less.

While I was on my travels, I hadn't consciously missed Mom. It was only when I came home, and when she was in talking distance, that I realised how subliminally she had been in my thoughts. My regular Mom phone calls were always made after six o'clock, the cheap-rate time, for Mom's sake rather than for my own. Mom's sense of economy never left her. She would have taken offence at anyone's extravagance on her behalf. But I needed to talk to her, to hear her voice, so to hell with the cheap-rate time. I dialled her number. It was early morning, and when she heard my voice at that hour she panicked.

'What's the matter?'

'Nothing,' I assured her. 'I just got back and I wanted to talk to you. I couldn't wait till six o'clock.'

She calmed down and slowly indicated her pleasure on hearing from me. She wanted to know about my trip and I gave her a précis account.

'Travel is exciting,' she said.

'You should do it, Mom,' I told her. 'Go to Boston and see Auntie Ray and Sylvie.'

'Well now you're back, perhaps I will,' she said, as if one of us had to stay here to look after the home. Then I really began to miss her.

'I'm coming down to see you,' I said. My feet were itchy enough for that kind of journey.

I decided to go down by train. Driving down the M4 is very boring. I hated crossing the Severn Bridge to be assaulted by signs in Welsh giving me directions. It was a farce. I was entering a part of a country where you'd be just as likely to hear French spoken in the subtitled streets, as you would Welsh. So I went down by train to avoid the captions, though they begin again at Cardiff station. I resent them less now. I simply regard them as pathetic. I didn't know the Welsh word for Taxi, but it didn't hinder me from finding one, and Mom was waiting on the doorstep when I arrived, having prepared a tasty supper.

I was so happy to be with her but I was still nervous. I wondered what there was about me that she could still disapprove of. I had done reasonably well in my career. I had got into the habit of combing my hair, and she wasn't to know whether or not I was keeping my drawers tidy. Yet I expected some reprimand or another. I was still desperate for her approval. But as it turned out, during the whole of my visit she did nothing but praise me, and even one morning when I had allowed my locks a respite – and how gratefully they had welcomed the non-combing – she made no comment. Her forbearance unnerved me. I was not used to such tolerance. I was happy for her, but bewildered too, for I did not know what facts had engineered such a change. Slowly I discovered them and they had nothing to do with her children. She had other concerns.

Over the week that I was with her, we talked about Israel's incursions into Lebanon, her nagging concern, as well as my own. All her life she had worked for Zionism. She and Pop had spent their weekends collecting door-to-door for projects in the Promised Land. Her pet project had been the baby home in Jerusalem, and to this end she organised tombolas, fairs, raffles and coffee mornings, and she was still doing so. But the news that was filtering out of the Promised Land was anything but promising.

'I'm glad Pop isn't here to see it,' she said.

The phrase, 'The God that failed' came into my mind and I understood the pain she felt; the disillusion, the helplessness. So she was busying herself, even more than she did in her younger days.

'They still need the baby home,' she said.

So together we went collecting.

'It's harder now,' she said. 'People are worried about Israel's future.'

She had arranged a coffee morning during my stay. I talked to the women who came. Women like Mom who all their lives had worked in the Zionist movement, and warily, shyly, they voiced their views, their fears and criticisms, and all in a whisper, fearful that others might hear. There were about two dozen of them, mostly women, and many, like Mom, widowed, and thankful that their husbands did not live to see the state Israel was in. They wouldn't fob themselves off with thoughts of the baby home. Important as it was, it would not blind them to the plight of Palestinian babies and, dare they utter it, the oppressive Israeli rule. As they spoke, they knitted. All the time. Baby clothes, booties, rompers, in a stubborn effort to confirm the importance of their project. But they had every right to criticise, every right to abhor such oppression, because in the past they had applauded the achievements of the Promised Land. And there were many. Democracy, to start with. The cultivation of every inch of land. The establishment of a trade union movement, a national health service, free education, care for the aged and new immigrants. There was much to applaud. And because they had admired it in the past, they had every right now to disapprove and to protest. They talked about the growth of anti-Semitism, and how in many cases the new label of anti-Zionism was simply a cover for what was innately anti-Semitic, but with its new tagging could pass as respectable. It was a lively discussion and I was glad that

Mom was still so deeply involved. A collection was made and receipts offered.

The following day I returned to London. I took an early train, one that would be crowded. I needed anonymous company. It's only when surrounded by people that I can feel truly alone. I managed to get a seat facing the engine. Had one such seat not been available, I would have stood for the whole journey rather than sit with my back to the engine. Pop was the same. So is Mom. It's a Jewish thing, I think, a post-holocaust compulsion. You must sit facing the engine, so that you can see where you are going. I settled myself in a corner seat. The noise around me, the chatter, the laughter, did not trouble me. I was replaying my visit to Mom, replaying her concerns and those of her friends. For they were my concerns too. Not only for the future of Israel, but the growth of anti-Semitism worldwide. And I recalled Leipzig.

Leipzig was many years ago, but the memory of its event was unerasable. I had just joined the band of documentary film-makers. Those were heady days for documentary, with the Post Office, the Coal Board and the Central Office of Information sponsoring their own films. Even without television sponsorship, there was no shortage of work, or of festivals to screen them. I was invited to join a group of documentary film-makers who were taking part in the Leipzig festival. This was in the days before the Wall came down and Leipzig lay in the Eastern region of the German Democratic Republic, under the uncomfortable rule of Soviet occupation. Most of the participants in the festival were from the Eastern bloc, though some token

English had been invited, as well as some Americans. I was new to the game and I was in awe of some of the names. Richard Leacock, Robert O'Flaherty's cameraman Basil Wright, Paul Rotha, the Maysel brothers from the States and John Grierson, king of them all.

We boarded an Aeroflot flight at Heathrow. I reckoned on a two hour or so journey to Leipzig and settled down with a book. It was a silent journey. There was little bonhomie among the crew. The stewardesses were very fat and surly, and they had to walk sideways through the aisle. The food, such as there was, was inedible. I fell asleep, and on waking, my watch indicated that we'd been in the air for just over four hours. We waited for some communication from the cockpit. When it came, it ordered us to 'distinguish' our cigarettes. Soon we would be landing in Warsaw. We learned later that the East German airport had been closed for repairs. We were given a meal at the airport – stuffed cabbage, as I remember, and stuffed something else. A stuffed apple followed and, almost fatally stuffed, we were herded into the station and onto a train. I was fast losing my appetite for any kind of festival and my mood was not improved by the thought that we were travelling on the very same track that had cattle-trucked hundreds of thousands of Jews to Auschwitz. I wondered why the railway lines were not screaming.

Leipzig was generous in its welcome and the festival was a happy time. The films had a distinctly DDR flavour, but some shunned propaganda yet had managed to gain a screening. I met a number of East German film-makers, most of whom have never been heard of since.

From the beginning of the week, I noticed that I was being followed. And not at all subtly. My stalker was clearly not a film-maker. With his gaunt looks and rimless spectacles, he came right out of central casting (spy section). At screenings he sat behind me, and in the bar he breathed down my neck. It did not surprise me that I was being tailed. I'd never kept my anti-Stalinist views quiet. But the man was beginning to get on my nerves. One time he followed me into a lift and we were alone.

'D'you speak English,' I asked him.

He seemed eager for communication.

'Yes,' he said.

'Well fuck off,' I told him.

After that he left me alone, and I feared for his future with the Stasi.

During the course of the week, we were offered a sightseeing tour. Most of the participants opted for the coach trip to Dresden. I asked the head gaffer to arrange a trip for me to Buchenwald. I set off with my silent driver. I had done my Buchenwald homework, I knew what had happened there, but I didn't know what to expect. Buchenwald was not a death camp. There were no ovens there. It was a labour camp, built from scratch by prisoners of different colours. The homosexual pinks, the politico blacks, and the yellow-starred Jews. The latter comprised the main body of the work force. Thousands of people died in the building of Buchenwald, many from hunger and work fatigue, or impatiently shot for their lack of skill. After the war, the camp was razed to the ground, but its symbols were retained; the eating halls, the so-called surgeries, the sleeping areas and work places. And of course the ornate gates proclaiming on the arch, '*Arbeit Macht Frei*'. But work didn't bring freedom in that place. It brought death.

My guide explained the layout of the camp and then he took me to the Museum built on the perimeter, a museum that supposedly commemorated the dead. My German was good enough to read and understand the captions of the exhibits. Photographs, personal effects, letters and sundry souvenirs. What struck me most during my museum wandering was that the word '*Jude*' never appeared. Yet it was well enough known through the listings of names in the Yad Vashem Museum in Jerusalem that hundreds of Jews had died in Buchenwald. On our way out of the museum, I asked my guide what sort of people had lived and died in the camp.

'Good German communists,' he told me.

'Only those? No Jews?'

He laughed. 'Absolutely not,' he said. 'That was a fairy tale. Just good German communists.'

It would be fruitless to argue with him. He was a young man brainwashed by the Soviet occupation. What depressed me even more was the sight of a crocodile line of German schoolchildren, batches of whom, I was told, made regular visits. It was part of their education in German history. And all they would gather were lies and more lies, with access to no evidence to expose those falsehoods they were fed. And as I sat on the train back to London after that visit to Mom, cautiously facing the engine, I wondered how those children had grown and whether now, in a united Germany, they were part of the right, venting the Jew-hatred that had been their mothers' milk.

Those women at Mom's coffee morning had cause enough for concern. I knew that the present day anti-Semitism was closely related to events in Israel. But most of that feeling was there anyway, and always had been. Anti-Semitism is a very light sleeper, and Israel, under its present government, had served as a certain and sure alarm clock. Its policies are indefensible. I thought of my friends in Israel, members of the Peace Now movement, and tried to imagine their despair. I honour those soldiers who refused to serve in the occupied territories, but there was little cause for hope. I found myself thinking like Mom. They will always need a baby home in Jerusalem.

Back in London, I was due to teach a creative writing class at Ty Newydd in North Wales. My co-teacher was Beryl Bainbridge as it always was. We'd got into the habit of doing gigs together. I'd met Beryl many years before on a trip to Israel – a writers' tour with Melvyn Bragg, Fay Weldon, William Trevor, the late Ted Willis, Iris Murdoch and John Bayley. Beryl and I made up the party. I confess that I didn't enjoy it very much. I felt decidedly an outsider. Yet it marked the beginning of a friendship that has endured for many years. We have much in common, Beryl and I. Children, grandchildren, and failed marriages. When we meet, we talk about everything except writing. We gossip, we keep each other abreast on the soaps to which we are both addicted, and we share our doubts about the benefits of such courses.

The whole business started in America. The idea that creative writing could be taught is faintly preposterous, and crazy enough for the American universities to give it a whirl. American academe is not afraid of getting egg on its face. Slowly the notion crossed the pond, and raised eyebrows. The English are pretty picky about their own great novelist tradition. This generates a reverence that is wary of experiment. The Americans are hampered less by tradition. Some of their great writers are barely out of copyright. They have no Dickens or Eliot breathing down their necks, and Faulkner's breath is still warm. Awe does not stifle them, one of the reasons perhaps why the modern American novel is far more audacious and exciting than its English counterpart.

Many people are intrigued by the magic of creative writing and wish to play a part in it. In England, the Arvon Foundation are pioneers in the field, and run creative writing sessions that are always over-subscribed. Following their lead, many libraries and universities now engage writers-in-residence, though the job usually turns out to be less of a sinecure than the writer had hoped. I have a friend who was once awarded one of these paid posts. He was cock-a-hoop. He was halfway through a novel at the time and he welcomed the opportunity to be freed of family responsibilities for a while, to devote himself entirely to finishing his book. After two solid months he returned home with not one extra word written. He was not to know that in the bottom drawers of his parish there lurked many an unfinished novel, poem or play, craving an airing, and he was suddenly deluged by an avalanche of hopeful and often hopeless words. But though still only halfway through his novel, he told me he'd learned something about the teaching of the craft. The grammar of writing is teachable, he said; the problems of structure for example, and plotting, the timing of the climax, the exact measuring of the denouement. I agreed with him. When talking to aspiring novelists I have found that structuring is a common problem. I've tried experimenting with the *Rashomon* effect, that is telling the same story from the different views of its characters. Often the results have proved more exciting than the original story. So too with experiments in the timing of climaxes, which sometimes result in astonishing changes in narrative, even to the extent of turning a tragedy into a farce. All the time we are exploring possibilities, seeking alternatives and this in itself is a creative pursuit. This is the basic grammar of writing. Totally teachable and shareable. But there is more to a novel than mere grammar.

There is music. I am astonished at the lack of music in the contemporary English novel. I read many and I am stunned by the sheer tone-deafness of the writing. The inability to hear the exact cadence, the exact harmony. The deafness to poetic rhythms, to the weight and thrill, for example, in a well-placed spondee. The acid test for a good piece of writing is that it may be read aloud and its harmonies heard. Good writing, even if its subject is violence or cruelty, should make one's ears water. What finally makes a good novel though, has little to do with these extras, any more than the composition of a piece of music has to do with a knowledge of harmony and counterpoint. More is needed. Imagination, and lunacy. Both unteachable.

When I teach such a course, I hope to transfer some of my own pleasure in writing to the students. I hope to demythologise the novelist's pursuit, to insist that it is a job like almost any other, and that the magic moments are few and far between. You must, of course, have something to say and the wherewithal to say it. Don't worry if it has been said before. Everyone's imagination is unique, and if *you* haven't said it, it has not been said before. But hardest of all, you must have self-discipline. To write a novel you must sit down and stay sitting. Unless you're a Hemingway and you stay standing. Or a Proust and you stay in bed. Then one word will generate another and likewise sentence after sentence, and that which you have written for no rhyme or reason on page three will find its astonishing logic twenty pages later. And that is a magic moment worth waiting for.

We do not talk about these things, Beryl and I, on our way to North Wales. No doubt she too is thinking about them. At the time we were concerned that we would miss out on episodes of our favourite soaps and hoped that our children would watch them for our subsequent benefit. But one soap we would not miss, for it is a late night one, *Prisoner Cell Block H*. We were looking forward to it, as a break from the reading of sundry manuscripts.

It's a long journey up to Bangor and we waited to catch sight of the sea at Colwyn Bay which is close to our station. As a born Cardiffian, I know that North Wales is quite a different country from the South. First of all, they speak Welsh there, always have done. They don't even bother with English subtitles. They look with no longing over the border. They prefer the leek to the rose. They are Plaid Cymru through and through, and like all intense patriotism, it smacks of elitism.

The creative writing course takes place in the village of Llanystumdwy and is housed in the former dwelling of David Lloyd George. It's a beautiful house with spacious grounds and there are small chalets alongside the house where the tutors are accommodated. Beryl and I shared a two-bedroomed bungalow with its own kitchen for late-night snacks and, most important of all, a television. We tested that it was in working order and we looked forward to Wednesday evening when we would be served with our *Cell Block H* fix.

There were about eleven people enrolled on the course, ten of them women. And there was Tom. Tom was known to both Beryl and me. He had, as it were, form. He was known to attend many writing courses and to bring with him the same half-finished novel every time. Tom was an amiable man and fitted well into the group, but nobody understood why he was there. For he rarely attended any of the classes, and heeded no advice from the tutors. He came solely for the end of the week joint recitals, when each student would read what he or she had accomplished during the week. It was then that Tom came into his own. He would insist on reading last, and when his turn came he read slowly and well and with great passion. But I have learned not to be fooled by good reading. Some of the best writers read appallingly. Tom was having his day though. Beryl and I had heard it before and exactly that same passage. We applauded him and he was pleased. His mission had been accomplished.

I always looked forward to a teaching course, and always with the hope of making a discovery. But this time, there was nobody's name with which I could run back to my agent or publisher to report a find. In fact the group, though charming and friendly, were a pretty talentless lot, but writing clearly gave them pleasure, and they seemed unimpeded by ambition.

On the Wednesday after supper, Beryl and I returned to our chalet and made our cocoa to have in front of the television. We had time to recap with each other on the matter of last week's episode. It had finished on a cliffhanger and we were waiting patiently for its resolution. When it began we were bewildered. The screen featured characters we'd never seen before. They were clearly uniformed screws of the prison. The opening scene was set in the cemetery of the prison grounds. A few inmates hovered on the rim. None of them seemed very moved. A priest was intoning the burial service but gave no clue as to whose dust was going to dust. We recognised a few faces, but they all seemed to have aged considerably. It seemed that we had missed out on at least a year's worth of episodes. Little old Bangor was streets ahead of London. Thereafter we had to give up on our favourite soap on our trips together, and strangely enough we didn't miss it. We could still depend on *EastEnders* and *Coronation Street* for our soap addiction.

So it was back to London and the cruddy gas stove that could no longer be ignored. Belsize was a basement flat and I longed for a little more light. So I swapped my hole in the ground for a hole in the sky, and I moved to a loft apartment in my old NW6 hunting ground to be closer to family. I loved it on sight. It had a studio room large enough to accommodate many grand pianos and the light was dazzling. Its present owner was moving out of the country. When I went to see her to make final arrangements I said, 'I can't wait to move in', to which she replied, 'And I can't wait to move out'. I was not to know that six years later I would have exactly the same conversation with a prospective buyer. For in truth, I couldn't wait to get out. It had been a mistake.

When I'd bought the flat, it didn't trouble me that it was a walk-up of four storeys. That is, not until I went travelling or shopping and had to lug the bags skyward. Yet when I finally regained my breath, I had happy times in loft land. I settled in and managed to complete three novels in that hole in the sky, and the oven crud never caught up with me. But I wasn't depending on the crud for my next move. It would be the breath, and the running out thereof.

When the call came to spend four weeks in Singapore teaching at the university in 1993 I was relieved, for whatever Singapore didn't have, it surely had lifts. And as it turned out, lifts were about the only benefit it offered. We flew Cathay Pacific. Just before landing, the pilot warned passengers that the possession of drugs was viewed as a capital offence in the country. There was a sudden rush to the lavatories and a frantic stuffing in the backs of seats, a source of great profit, no doubt, to those privileged to clean the aircraft after landing.

Singapore is a terrible place. A police state par excellence. Yet apart from the traffic cops, there are few policemen to be seen. But they are there all right, and plenty of them. In civilian clothes. The island is fervent in its belief in capital punishment. Per capita, it has the highest rate of execution in the world. The cat-o-nine tails is pretty busy as well. Singaporeans will point out in their defence that it is the safest place in the world, that a woman can walk alone in the darkest places without fear. It seemed to me that capital punishment was still too high a price to pay for such security.

Between teaching sessions, I behaved like a tourist. I wandered around the supermarkets. It is seldom in such shops that one does not see a handicapped child or a wheelchair customer. But they are absent in Singapore. There are no facilities for the handicapped, no ramps, no special toilets or transport aids. The disabled are hidden. They have to stay at home. And God help you, if you are an outed homosexual, for which you will earn a lashing that is supposed to make you see the error of your wayward ways.

The government is obsessed with litter. A dropped piece of paper in the street is punishable, yet there are few places where one can put one's rubbish. As a result, it is common to take the short bus ride into Malaysia and dump it over the border. Towards the end of my stay, I had accumulated enough waste to merit a journey to the frontier town. While on the bus I noticed many Singaporeans who, with their plastic bags, were clearly on the same mission as myself. On arrival we had to go through customs. The official looked at my passport, scanning every overloaded page. Then he told me I could not enter the country. I was furious. What with South Africa and the Soviet Union, I was beginning to think I ought to change my toothpaste. I asked him why. With unveiled contempt, he pointed to two Israeli stamps of entry. 'Not allowed,' he said. A good place to leave rubbish, I thought, and I dumped it surreptitiously on my way back to the bus.

I was glad to leave Singapore and I am not likely to return. So it was back to climbing the four flights again, though after Singapore, it no longer seemed so burdensome.

PART SEVEN

The most attractive feature of my hole in the sky was the top floor studio. It was a room built for chamber music, and it is there where I spent some of my happiest hours. I didn't have to look around for players. Between the family we could cater for duets, trios, quartets, and for the great C major Schubert an extra cellist was always available. But that was rare. We stuck mainly to family. And they were very tolerant. I was the only non-professional among them and they seemed happy to make allowances. After every session, when they had all gone home, I started to practise, determined to make a better show of myself next time. But such practice always left me depressed, seething with 'if onlys'. Then I would go back to whatever novel I was working on, aware that writing had always been, and ever would be, a second choice. I suppose that this thought has dogged me ever since I picked up a pen, and it is forever followed by a bout of low spirits. Nothing as radical as depression. Rather a sense of frustration that is slow to crumble. In the early days I looked for someone to blame, the easiest way of explanation. But as it turned out, the most futile. The target of my blame was Mom. Who else? Not for specifics, just her as a person, and all her expectations and constant disapproval. But it was not until I myself was a mother that I realised, possibly out of self-defence, that seeking to blame is a sterile pursuit. And blaming others stunts one's own growth.

I recall a specific incident. My daughters were 'teenaging' and it was a difficult time. Their demands were constant and my refusals likewise. Rudi was rarely around while I was giving him his requested 'time'. One day, when the girls were at the end of their tether, and I at mine, I shouted at them, 'I didn't invent motherhood, you know'. At that moment, with gale force, the idea struck me that I had a mother too, and so did Grandma, and so back and back in expectational and disapproving time. I think that was the moment when I began to forgive, and since that time I've not sought to blame, and I feel it as a kind of liberation. Now I recall Mom for her virtues, for that love and gentleness she was able to show her grandchildren. Sharon, being the first of that brood, was always her favourite. Sharon was my first child and, as such, she bore the brunt of all my expectations, for I was not Mom's daughter for nothing. She was nine years old and at George Eliot primary school when her headmaster suggested she should undergo an IQ test. He was much impressed with her. I should not have listened to him, but I did. I took her to a day-long testing. I quote the letter of her results.

'Sharon made an exceptionally high score, giving a mental age of sixteen years ... This ranking places her among the 1 per cent of the population who can be classed as of very superior intelligence ... It is inevitable that such a child must present an educational problem, since her interests and her abilities must place her far above the rest of the class ... She will need wise handling.'

And by God, they were right. I had always thought she was bright, but I was her mother after all and to have it so authentically confirmed only served to increase my expectations. And they did her no favours. I was a loving mother, but I did not love wisely, and I have never ceased to regret the mistakes I made in her upbringing. Her school career was erratic. She was easily bored, and thus disruptive. Slowly she settled and went to York University where she read Music, her passion and her talent. She played the harp in the university orchestra, sang in every choir and has since earned a living as a musician.

Meanwhile Rebecca jogged along, relatively unfettered. Her passion is painting and sculpture, and after her A levels, she went to St Martin's School of Art and Design. But after a year, she dropped out and joined fringe theatre, a group called 'Beryl and the Perils'. Eventually she returned to sculpture and found her own studio. She is drawn to animals, and had a small success with an enterprising council, Brent, who commissioned four five-metre steel giraffes, and they stand on the corner of Harrow

Road and Scrubbs Lane tottering on high heels, while
their heads and long eyelashes flutter in the wind. There
followed a commissioned ostrich for Queen's Park, and
this too was constructed of steel. In search of a further
commission, Rebecca sculpted a large white egg and
placed it beside the ostrich. Then she went to Brent
Council and told them the good news. 'It's bound to
hatch,' she said, and suggested a commission for a baby
ostrich. But the borough of Brent is not into propagation,
and the egg remains undisturbed. But it will hatch, of
course, Brent Council or no Brent Council, or so Rebecca
believes.

Mom continued to live in the old family house in Cardiff.
And alone. But Beryl was near, back in her home town
after marriage, children and years in New York. She had
married an American. They'd met at the Tanglewood
Music Festival where Beryl was playing. They'd set up a
chicken farm in the Borscht Belt in Glen Wild, but the
farm was unprofitable and they decided to move back to
New York. However selling the farm was not straightfor-
ward. When the wind was blowing from a certain
direction, the smell from a neighbour's silo was excruciating. So they had to resort to hourly weather forecasts
before they could invite would-be buyers to view. One day
the wind was fair, and so was a buyer, and the deal was
done. I often visited them in New York and spent happy
times with them and their children.

The violin still played a major part in Beryl's life and
continued to do so as the children grew, and left home –

as did their father. Every year, Beryl came back to Cardiff
to be with Mom and the family. One year on the Cardiff
train, she sat next to a man who was carrying a violin. It
was natural that they fell into conversation. He told her
that he was a violinist in the Welsh National Opera
orchestra, and that they had a vacancy for a fiddler. Beryl
decided to audition. It took some nerve because her playing experience was chamber music and orchestral. She had
never set eyes on an opera score. But she practised and
practised and practised, while Mom expected and disap-
proved on the sidelines. But Mom was proud and happy
when Beryl got the job, and she shared her pride with her
friends.

Mom's social circle was slowly shrinking. She was well
into her eighties, and many of her contemporaries had
died. Who was left of the Cohen brood? Auntie Annie had
died in Grandma's wake. Auntie Beattie too, leaving her
man of the cloth to his own congregation hopping. Uncle
Hymie, he who was going to fend for them all but didn't,
died, possibly because he wanted to. My two hijacked
aunts still flourished in Boston, Massachusetts, though
their abductor had long since passed on, no doubt from
sheer exhaustion. But Mom was the only one left in
Cardiff – since Uncle Monty, the youngest had died. Of
course, he had already lain with the dead, so when he was
taken very ill I took myself down to Cardiff.

He was in his early seventies, and because of his war
wounds nobody had expected him to live that long. And
since he had so steadfastly defied all prognosis, it seemed
almost offensive to find himself in a moribund state. He

chose to believe his doctor who assured him that he would pull through. Not only that, he urged him to stop smoking. It would help his condition, he said, though he could see that his patient was clearly at death's door. Now my Uncle Monty had smoked nearly all of his life, chain-smoked almost. He'd even reached for a fag in that long-ago morgue. Smoking was his pleasure, his relief, his painkiller, his comfort. Yet such was the innocent faith he placed in that stupid doctor that he gave it up. Cold-turkeyed after so many nicotine years. After three smokeless and agonising days, he died.

During Uncle Monty's time in hospital, Auntie Sophie, his wife, was staying in Mom's house, together with their two children. They visited him daily. I was worried about Auntie Sophie. Theirs had been a difficult marriage; it was more a battleground than a union. His tempers erupted out of his pain, and his wife was his temper-target. Yet I think they must have loved each other. Auntie Sophie was a shy woman who, without being a victim, accepted her lot. She understood his pain, and in its name she made daily allowances. She spent most of her time at the hospital bed and returned at night exhausted and bewildered. I stayed in the house with Mom. We didn't go to visit him, we felt that his dying was a close family matter. But one day, his last, Auntie Sophie came home early. She was exhausted, she said. But she was too anxious to sleep. For almost an hour she sat bolt upright, and didn't utter a word. She was waiting for the phone to ring. When it did she let out a small cry, which could have been a sob or a titter. I should have answered the phone but Mom beat me to it, and I was grateful. I held Auntie Sophie's hand, though I'm sure she didn't feel my touch. I tightened my grip, but her hand was numb. Soon Mom returned and held her.

'I wish you long life,' she said, that traditional Jewish comfort to the bereaved. 'I'll make the arrangements.' And she was gone again.

It is a Jewish custom to bury the dead quickly. Uncle Monty would be interred the following day. We sat in silence. Auntie Sophie did not cry. She sat zombie-like, as if no part of her was alive at all. Mom asked me to make tea and I was glad of an excuse to leave the silence. We had a whistling kettle, and when the water came to the boil I suppose the hissing noise must have drowned Auntie Sophie's last offended cry. I heard Mom calling and I rushed back to the room. Mom was crouched over Auntie Sophie who lay on the floor, still as a stone. Dead as dead could be.

'What happened?' I asked.

'Heart, I suppose,' Mom said. 'She went into a spasm. And she screamed. That was all.'

'I'll ring the doctor,' I said. I had to make sure that she was dead.

But Mom had no doubts. She called the doctor anyway and then made another call. I reckoned it was to the Rabbi, with whom she was probably ordering a double.

The doctor lost no time in confirming what we already knew.

'It was swift,' he said, by way of consolation. 'But it wasn't a heart attack.'

That was just an excuse. Auntie Sophie had died of simple submission. In the face of Uncle Monty's final assault, she had capitulated. She could not wake the battleground, empty of a beloved enemy. She had simply turned the other cheek and surrendered.

When the doorbell sounded, Mom rushed to answer. It would be the children returned from the hospital. She would wish them long life on the doorstep, twice over she would wish it for them, as a way of softening the blow. They would be prepared. They rushed into the room, infected carriers from one deathbed to another. Perhaps they thought that they could save her and thus cleanse themselves. They caught their mother's bewildered look, then shared it between them. Thenceforth, they would never be able to understand anything at all.

I stayed in Cardiff for the *Shiva*, the seven days of mourning. A synagogue clerk delivered three low chairs for the principal mourners. He'd prepared for four, until the second telephone call. I recalled the mourning for Pop when all the mirrors in the house had been shrouded in sheets, and I did the same for Uncle Monty and Auntie Sophie. After the funeral, people visited with dishes of food, and in the evening men came to say prayers. I found that *Shiva* soothing. I enjoyed the ritual of it, the prescribed mourning time, the limit on bereavement but no boundaries on grief. When it was over I took Mom back to London, and for a whole peaceful week not a syllable of disapproval escaped her. But it was a high price to pay for her silence.

*

It had been three novels since I last moved. My oven could easily have coped with another two. So there was no move compulsion on its behalf. But I was tired of traipsing up the four flights, especially when burdened with shopping or luggage. Besides, I felt the need for a garden. Not that I am by any means a gardener, but I longed for some outside space. I wanted to sit in the sun when it shone, and to boast a washing line with sheets flying. So began yet another search. My friends feared for my sanity. I was not a shaker, but I was certainly a mover. I had to convince them that I *liked* moving, that moving house was the surest route to dispossession, which is surely a measure of one's own growth.

I had no difficulty in selling my loft, so in June 2001 I was able to buy without delay. I wanted to stay in the neighbourhood, in violin distance of Cyril and a piano call from Harold. So I moved literally around the corner to a ground floor flat with a large garden. And it is here that I presently write, though I make no promises to myself, oven or no oven, that I will not move again.

At the time, I'd made some surprise money from an American sale. I decided to blow it. Occasionally I'd had dreams of a second home in the sun. I wanted it for myself, but mainly for my family, and I had visions of my grandchildren disporting themselves in Grannie's folly. So I set off to Majorca. I made a number of trips, often sponsored by shady agents who went out of business even before a deal could be done. But through their auspices, I was able to tour the whole island. I fell in love with Valdemosa where Chopin drove Georges Sand round the bend, but it was too far from the sea. Then there was Deya, Robert Graves's hideout, and though there was sea there, it was difficult to reach. So I settled for the south-west area which was but a half hour's drive from the airport.

It was in Santa Ponsa, a kiss-me-quick place, and common as muck. But it must have answered some latent need of mine. It was slap bang on the sea, and with a pool to boot. A two-bedded flat with plenty of room for sleeping bags. A supermarket was directly opposite and any number of bars. There were fish and chip shops run by running ex-pats, and in frequent change of ownership. But the light on the island was dazzling and I couldn't wait to land in Palma just for the sight of it. I went there often, sometimes just for the weekend, and I lent the keys to friends who used it as much as I. Once I went there during an early spring. A summer heat and light greeted me. It was early morning, about seven o'clock, and I went swimming in a blue and empty sea. After a shower, I went to a local bar for a coffee. It was already packed with British tourists because it offered a full English breakfast. Not a word of Spanish could be heard. I asked for my regular *cortado*, and although I'm not a drinker by nature I ordered a cognac to go with it. This, at nine o'clock in the morning. I was in danger of turning into a typical ex-pat. It was a glaring red light. That dream of mine of a place in the sun could well become the stuff of nightmares. I decided to sell my kiss-me-quick abode and it was swiftly snapped up by an English plumber who was an ex-pat by nature and only needed a simple change of address to legitimise his status. So I returned to my garden and the local pool, and I imagine the light and the sun.

I was about to publish one of my novels. It was a bad habit of mine, but I had little else to do. I recalled the publication of my first book, and the excitement and trepidation that attended it. My publishers promised me that in the fullness of time they would send me copies of all my reviews. But I was impatient. So I subscribed to Durrants Press Agency and waited for the post. It trickled in timidly. The agency was thorough. Even a mention in the *Cornish Gazette* merited their attention. But my overall catch was puny. Then one morning the postman rang my bell and offered me a Durrants' package that required extra postage. I paid with pleasure. It was a bulky affair and the thought crossed my mind that I had arrived. A villa on the Riviera loomed large. Bonjour Mr Greene. Bonjour Mr Maugham.

I opened the package carefully and slowly, to savour my success, and I read. Cutting after cutting. Of Rubens, without a doubt. But not yours truly. Peter Paul it was, who at that time was enjoying a grand exhibition at the Royal Academy. I cancelled my subscription and thereafter have nurtured a faint suspicion of reviews in general. Over the years I have lost interest in them. And I am glad of it. I see some of my writer friends lose sleep over poor reviews, and even send hate mail to those reviewers. I am thankfully saved all that, for unless a review accidentally comes into my hands, I don't read them. I have had rave reviews in my time, and savage ones too. But I am indifferent to both. I have never gained any constructive criticism from either. I know whether a book of mine works or not, and I don't need a reviewer to tell me. I bear no grudge against reviewers; there are good among them, and bad. But there are good and bad novelists too. Everyone has to earn a living.

At the time, I was making frequent visits to Cardiff. Occasionally I went to dress rehearsals of the Welsh Opera Company, and if I stood on tip-toe I could catch a glimpse of Beryl in the pit. In 1984 they were rehearsing *Don Giovanni*. It's a work I listen to often and I know it well, and it was pleasing to see that Beryl was part of it. Elvira was singing '*Mi tradi quell'alma ingrata*'. She has some of the finest arias in the work, yet as a character she's a right old pain in the arse. She reminds me of myself and my doormatishness. But she was singing like an angel.

My relationship with Mom was easier in those days. She had mellowed, and though ageing she still worked and begged for the Jerusalem baby home, and tried not to be anxious about other Israeli matters. And it was almost time to celebrate her. She was soon going to be ninety years old. She used to say 'The days go so slowly, but the weeks fly. And so do the years.' Though she was ageing, she looked young enough. Her face was unlined and her thick white hair shone with curls. When she was eighty, she lied about her age, lopping off five years or so, to suit her appearance. But as she approached ninety she lied in reverse, boasting of her years. I heard her once admit to ninety-five and she rejoiced in the incredulous amazement of her listener. 'You don't look a day over seventy,' her friend told her. Another liar, but both women were comfortable with their falsehoods. Anyway, whatever Mom said, and whatever anyone else supposed, she knew from her birth certificate of 26 March 1893 that she was a decade away from the Queen's telegram, and so did we. And we decided to celebrate her.

It occasioned a gathering of the clan. My two hijacked aunts flew in from Boston. They were very different from Mom. Always had been, I suppose. Because they lived in America they thought that they were sophisticated. They measured such sophistication in terms of central heating, power showers, air conditioning, all of which Mom had lived her life without. But despite the differences, they were still very close. I listened to them as they listed the separate states of their health. Auntie Ray offered a knee problem, and Aunty Sylvie a dicey hip. Mom could offer nothing in the surgery department, she admitted to simply ageing. But my aunts would have none of that. Though they were but a few years younger than Mom, ageing had nothing to do with them. It seemed that each of them was secretly vying to outlive the other. Yet they were happy together, the three of them.

I listened to their reminiscences. They talked only about the past. The future was unreliable, and in the present they had little in common. But the past belonged to each of them, and in different colours. I eavesdropped on their recall, and it occasioned much laughter between them. I was happy that they had come to celebrate. I knew that they would never come again and that their departure would be fraught. There would be long and silent looks between them, long and silent enough to imprint their images. Their farewells would have to be casual, as if they meant nothing at all.

Hugo came from New York, he was part of the clan after all. He had never lost touch with the family and had often visited. He had done well for himself, had prospered, and though he endured an unhappy marriage, he took much pleasure in his children. The other side of the family came too, Pop's side with which we'd had little contact in the past. Esther and Lena, my two cousins, daughters of Berl, Pop's brother. The Russians. Those whom Cyril had met in Moscow in their bugged apartment, fearful of uttering a syllable of dissent. By sundry means, more foul than fair, they had managed to get out and to settle in Israel, and now they lived in the Little Russia of Holon, a suburb of Tel Aviv. I had numerous cousins from Mom's side of the family and many of them were present. But I more than welcomed Esther and Lena. We did not exchange political views. Like many Russian immigrants to Israel they were solidly right-wing Likud. It was understandable – they had suffered years of left-wing oppression, and in their new home they had hopefully opted for the right. It would have been pointless to argue with them. It was in any case a family celebration, and it seemed that with their presence, Pop was suitably represented.

The gathering took place at Cyril's house since it was large enough to accommodate the tribe. Sharon had composed a song that celebrated Mom's ninety years. It is now Sharon's custom to mark significant family birthdays with a song and this was her first, one that is scored for a family orchestra. The family band has changed its tune with the times. Harold's grandchildren have contributed a cello, a violin and a clarinet. At Sharon's celebration of my recent birthday, alas Cyril was gone, but we had, in addition to the rest, Rebecca on banjo and my own grandchildren, Joshua on the cello and Dashiel on the saxophone. But on that occasion, other family members formed the choir and Sharon at the piano conducted:

There is no no nonagenarian like you, Dolly,
No less sheepish Arien than you, Dolly.

And Mom listened with pride and approval. It was a lavish feast, and all palates were catered for. Vodka for the Russians, sweet martinis for the 'sophisticates', and straight champagne for the natives. And of course there were speeches.

Pop was a great one for speeches. I remember how before every Zionist meeting where he was delegated to speak, he would light a fire for the sole purpose of burning his discards. Crunched paper after crunched paper would join the flames. His views on partition in Palestine. These varied between grudging approval and absolute promotion. The flames swallowed all his changes of mind. Then his contempt for revisionism. That never wavered. He raged at Jabotinsky – a dirty word from my childhood – who promoted an Israel on both sides of the Jordan. Pop would even dare to mention Palestinian rights. As I recalled his speech-making process, I knew that he would have been appalled at the present revisionist leanings in Israel and I was relieved he hadn't lived to see it. Yet another whose God had failed. But had he lived, he would, like Mom, have clung to his own version of a baby home.

Mom loved speechifying, and so did Beryl. But Harold played dumb, and Cyril hid in the cupboard. As for myself, I was equally tongue-tied. I had perforce made many speeches in my time. I had words in plenty for the state of contemporary English fiction, for creative writing in general, for the corrupt nature of some publishers and some agents. And for all forms of psychiatry. I could go to town on that one. But I couldn't stretch to a simple piece of celebration. So I passed, and Beryl took over. Beryl is the archivist in the family, the keeper of certificates, letters and photographs. She had done her homework and was able to chronicle Mom's life from its beginnings. Mom listened in bewildered recall. Then it was Mom's turn. She was gentle, mellow and a little tearful. Once on her feet, I did not think she would pass on an opportunity to promote the baby home. I just hoped she wouldn't stretch to asking for donations. She didn't. But in a way she did, for that was all that her speech implied. And she did indeed go back to Cardiff with a goodly sum for her pet project.

Shortly afterwards, Beryl retired from the opera and set about building a Suzuki practice at home in Cardiff. She is a wonderful teacher, and the house was filled with little people and their sometimes pushy parents. I think the noise got on Mom's nerves – there is a limit to the number of times one can listen to 'Twinkle, twinkle little star', a Suzuki player's debut piece – but she relished the children's company. Then Beryl needed to go to New York to attend her son's wedding. Mom was frail, too frail to come up to London, and at the time I was reading at the Adelaide Festival. So Beryl found a temporary home for her, a kind of sheltered hotel in the countryside close to Cardiff. When I returned from Australia I went straight to see her. It was a beautiful home, and Mom appreciated its luxuries. But she was not happy there. Her sight was failing, a sad deprivation for one who all her life had been such an avid reader. I had brought her one of my audio books but she refused to listen to the tapes. It would have been a kind of abdication.

'I want to go home,' she told me. 'If I stay here, with all their caring, I could live for ever. But I've had enough, Bern. I want to go home.'

I arranged for her return immediately, and stayed with her until Beryl came back from New York. Thereafter I went often to Cardiff, and so did my girls. Mom had a live-in carer, Pat, who tenderly held the fort to the strains of 'Twinkle, twinkle'. One weekend we all went down to see her. We sat on her bed, her four children, and held her hand. We talked about everything on earth that had nothing to do with her dying. Then it was she who swept away the irrelevant subjects. Her mind was crystal clear.

'I want to tell you something,' she said. 'Something you must always remember. I love you all. But more impor-tant, much more important is that I know that you all love me. And have shown me that love. So that when I have gone, none of you will have the right to feel guilty. I tell

you this so you won't have to mourn for long. For it is
guilt that prolongs grief.'

It's a phrase that I have never forgotten.

One day, soon afterwards, Beryl was teaching a Suzuki
class and Pat was taking Mom's breakfast to her room.
She was still sleeping, or so Pat thought. She tapped her
gently but there was no response. 'Mummy?' she whispered, perhaps remembering her own, long since gone.
'Mummy,' she called again, and louder this time. And
angrily, with that same anger of her own orphaned time.
It was clear that Mom had died, and hopefully painlessly
in her sleep. Pat was in a quandary. Should she interrupt
Beryl in her class, or should she wait until the children
went home? She decided to wait. Just another half hour,
she reckoned, and Mom couldn't be deader than she
already was. As Beryl closed the front door after her last
pupil, she made for the stairs.

'She gone,' Pat said. 'I didn't want to disturb you.'

A phrase for Beryl that she will never forget.

Mom was ninety-four years old when she died, and
some people thought it consoling to say that she'd had a
good innings. But a good innings is never good enough.
Sharon was inconsolable. I think she felt that she had lost
a mother. But as Mom had predicted, I didn't grieve. I
was simply stung. And to this day I miss her. I miss her
in the minutiae. I still reach for the phone at six o'clock,
the cheap rate time, to talk to her. And I wish she were
here to savour the good things. We erected a bench in the
rose garden of Waterloo Park, where she and Pop used to
love to walk. The dedication to them both is still readable,

though it is dotted with etched graffiti of 'Paul loves Linda' and 'John loves Richard', with kisses and hearts galore. I think Mom and Pop would approve of that. Whenever anything good happens to me, something praiseworthy perhaps, I ring Beryl and tell her to go to the rose garden and tell it to the bench. God help me, but I still need their approval.

PART EIGHT

Now we come to Cyril. It was in 1996 when Cyril died that I first thought of writing a memoir. When I write a novel I rarely plot, and unless it is based on a historical event I never know how a novel will end. But for a memoir it seemed to me that Cyril's death provided a logical ending. I couldn't believe that there would be anything more in my life that would be of equal importance to commit to memory. I was wrong of course. One is never let off the hook of memory. It can be a solace, a means of escape, and sometimes a damned inconvenience. But you can never rid yourself of it. It will haunt or comfort you till the day you die. There would be other events which would be recorded willy nilly.

So when does a memoir end? Logically, I suppose, when one loses one's memory. But I don't believe that that ever happens. Ever. And an incident on a visit to an old people's home confirmed that belief. I wrote a novel that was set in a retirement home for the aged. I recall visiting such a home in Cardiff and meeting with a lady who was in her seventies. I was taken to her room where she was sitting on the edge of her bed, sobbing. Between her cries I heard muttering, but I couldn't decipher her words. But whatever she was saying, the words were clearly breaking her heart. I waited. I waited long enough I suppose to declare that I was willing to listen. It seemed that little attention had been paid to her plight. After a while, she stopped crying and she stared at me. Then she spoke, in the whimpering tones of a child.

'They burned down Vati's store.'

She was from Germany, I knew, a refugee from long ago. It was a childhood memory of how they had burnt down her daddy's shop. She said it again and again, as if she'd said it many times before and nobody had believed her.

'Where was the shop?' I asked.

'They burned it down,' she said.

The shop's location was clearly irrelevant in her memory. It was the fire she saw, and seemed to feel even, so graphic was her recall. Later, her son came to visit her. I asked him about the incident and he confirmed it. His grandfather's shop, a haberdashery, had been burned down in Hamburg on *Kristallnacht*. He had learned of the fire from an uncle, but his mother had never mentioned it. Never. Perhaps she simply couldn't afford to recall it. Until now. It was probably Alzheimer's that had released that terror. Even in her mind's chaotic confusion, the fire would not be denied. No. One doesn't lose one's memory. Not in one's lifetime anyway.

So after Cyril's death, grievous as it was, there would be other events evoking recall.

He had spent forty years as a first fiddle player in the LSO and seventeen years as its board member. That little brother of mine to whom I'd passed the half-sized violin in my childhood. His favourite conductors were Pierre Monteaux, Celibidache, and Leonard Bernstein. He loved Mozart with a passion, and with an equal passion he loathed Mahler. He viewed Mahler's work as aural pornography. Claudio Abbado, who was the LSO conductor at the time of Cyril's retirement, and who knew of Cyril's Mahler aversion, gave him as a leaving present the score of Mahler's first symphony, and to off-set the leg-pull one of his own batons. Janet gave him a leaving party and most of the orchestral players partied with him. They gave him a computer, which Cyril regarded with thinly veiled bewilderment. But from time to time he still free-lanced with the orchestra, and he joined a scratch group of semi-retired musicians to journey to Bangkok to play for the King of Thailand's birthday. It was there that he became ill. On his return to London he was diagnosed with cancer of the pancreas and was given only a short time to live. He told Janet, then took her for a walk in Regent's Park. None of us believed it. Our anger left no room for belief. Yet as the weeks passed, the symptoms were undeniable. In time he was bedridden.

I sat by the bedside and talked to him. He was partially asleep. I touched his forehead and thought I saw him smile. His children, Emily and Saul, were lying either side of him holding his hands. Janet uncovered him. She thought he might be sweating. His body was yellow. I've always loved that colour. Although it is the colour of cowardice, it had nothing to do with Cyril. Cyril was a brave man, and often, in the face of disapproval, he spoke his mind. Fighting severe opposition, it was he who insisted on admitting women players as permanent members of the orchestra. No, cowardice was not for Cyril. But it is also the colour of memorial. I thought of the yellow ribbons that Americans pinned to trees in the name of those sons who had fallen in Vietnam. But memorial was not for Cyril either. That we would not acknowledge. Yellow was for the buttercup that Cyril placed under his chin as a little boy, to see whether he liked butter. Yellow was the school badge he won for cricket. Yellow was the colour of the silk scarf he laid over his violin. Yellow was life and pleasure for Cyril. His body had been cruelly misinformed. Janet lay by his side, and together they cradled him.

It was past midnight. I left them saying I'd be back in the morning. I was not in any way disturbed, I would see Cyril in the morning. There was no way I could accommodate any alternative. I went straight to bed and fell asleep almost immediately. Suddenly I woke. I looked at the clock, it was ten minutes past three. I got up, almost automatically, and I dressed. I felt the tears gathering behind my eyes, and I forced them to go back where they came from. The phone rang as I was putting on my coat. I knew it would be Janet. 'I'm on my way,' I told her.

Cyril had died at ten past three, and taken much of my *raison d'être* with him. I wondered at that unconscious connection, that exact synchronicity of our severance. It was a God-bothering moment. I have such moments occasionally. I have been an agnostic all my life, but I can't deny such moments. The sight of a zebra in a zoo, for example, will trigger one with the marvel of the symmetry of its stripes. Such a God-bothering moment can be inconvenient, for it defies any logical explanation. The stripes I can deal with, but the symmetry foxes me. Fearful, as Blake called his tyger. But what else is fear but belief.

But God, if He gives you a troubled thought, can sometimes be kind. I was in hospital with a threatening heart condition, and only much later did I learn that there had been fears for my recovery. I was confronted with all the signs of the seriousness of my condition but the very last thing on my mind, as a God-given gift perhaps, was the thought that I might not recover. My family were continually at my bedside, my daughters, sister, brother, my grandchildren, distant cousins. Friends came and went continually. And when I saw my publisher sitting at my bedside, that surely was incontrovertible proof of my impending demise. Yet God was good to me at that time, and kept me unaware of my condition. He was the same with Cyril. Cyril too was shown all the signs, but he talked of playing chamber music again and of going on holiday. It was a moment when God bothered him with kindness.

Cyril had a secular cremation, but a friend recited the

Kaddish, that traditional Jewish prayer for the dead. At his memorial, Saul played the Bach double with his teacher, and members of the orchestra played Mozart's clarinet quintet. It was a beautiful service but it afforded me little solace. Music in itself can do more than lighten the heart, but that day it had little strength to fight its heartbreaking context. I knew that such sorrow could be overcome. Adjustments could be made. Even to our erstwhile family quartet. We were now a trio, and we would have to play and listen to a very different melody.

I had begun seeing more of Rudi again. For the first time since our separation, he was alone. No woman had ever left him. It was he, who in a self-destructive mood, had abandoned each one of them. He had clearly chosen to live alone. This choice was no doubt prompted by the state of his health. He was not well. His heart was unreliable and his sight was failing. I had never lost the deep affection I had always felt for him. It annoyed me at times and often I tried to rid myself of it, but I held on to it, for to lose it would have seemed a negation of all those years I had spent with him. Unlike myself, he had not been blessed with a close family. His parents with whom he was always distant had died, and he saw little of Madi with whom he had nothing in common. He told me once that after our parting he sorely missed my tribe. But he had many friends, most of whom were painters whose careers, in some cases, he had enabled and encouraged. He loved paintings and he had begun to collect when we were first married. At first, the works of his friends. William Turnbull, Leon Kossoff, Patrick Caulfield, John Hoyland,

Euan Uglow. He was comfortable in the company of painters, and though he was a novelist, he was uneasy among writers. I wished he'd been a painter himself. Then the loss of language as a child would not have been so cruel an impediment. Though he wrote some memorable novels, especially his first, *The Hooligan*. It was a portrait of a German SS officer who worked in the camps, and explored such a man's psyche. It was a remarkable achievement for a twenty-three-year-old and it promised an extraordinary development. But he still dreamed in German, he told me, and it enraged him. Compared with the horrendous grief that the holocaust engendered, Rudi's loss of language was hardly worth a mention, but it left him with unerasable scars. I had always harboured these thoughts about Rudi, and in their name I made countless allowances. And although they cost me dear, I've never regretted them, especially when he was ill and needed my support. So I saw him often.

He had mellowed considerably, and he showed me a kindness that in the past he could never have afforded. One evening I phoned him, just to say hello, and he asked me if I could bring him some grapefruit juice. I bought four cartons from the local corner shop and went straight to his flat. He was grateful. He looked so ill, I couldn't bear his gratitude. It crossed my mind to offer to stay the night with him, but such an offer would have been loaded with God knows how many inferences, so I stayed with him for a while and then I left.

In the morning I went shopping, and when I came home there were three missed calls on my answering machine, but no messages had been left. I wondered about it, because it was rare that this occurred. Later on, I realised that the news that Rudi had died could hardly be left on an answering machine. When the phone rang again, I rushed to answer it. It was Sharon and she was crying.

'Rudi died this morning,' she said. 'We're at the flat.'

I drove up to Hampstead in a state of total mindlessness. Sharon met me at the door.

'K is here,' she said. She thought she ought to warn me. K, whom I had not laid eyes on for years, that woman for whom Rudi had left me, she who was the mother of his son. She of the colossal glasses and the boy bum. But I didn't give a toss who was there. I felt I was the only one who had the mourning rights for Rudi. Me and my two children. I went straight to the bedroom where he lay and I held his beautiful hands. I was sad, of course, but at the same time I was wondering what I ought to be feeling. I had spent all my grief on Cyril. And all my tears. What had I left for Rudi, save for an overwhelming regret? I know that time does heal, and that in Cyril's case time with its healing will serve me well. But Rudi was different. Time heals only if you give time, time. There is sometimes a need to hang on to one's sorrow, and I feared that, as far as Rudi was concerned, I would not give time its due. I had too many regrets and still too much rage to let time run its natural course. Rudi's death would take me much longer to accept with peaceful resignation. But as the years pass, I can recall with greater ease the good and happy times we spent together, and in their shadow the dark years fade.

I am a quarter of a century away from a telegram from the queen. Or from the king perhaps, or maybe even Camilla. It is two novels since I have last moved and I still have much to dispossess. But for the moment I shall ignore my oven, and make a start on my twenty-sixth novel.

It will be a story about writing a memoir. About the omissions that such a work entails. About the avoidance of hurt and thus the loss of certain events, for people are more important than literature. A story too, about self-restraint and self-deception, and about wisdom in hindsight. Above all, it will be a novel about the truth, the whole truth and nothing but the truth, and such a truth can be told only when cloaked in fiction. It will not be written in the first person, 'I'. In that thorny pronoun there is only the past. 'I' is final. 'I' is the recognition of death. No, the story will be told in the third person, the pronoun that is entitled to envisage a future. Yes, I shall start on it tomorrow, and in the morning I shall wake up and wonder what I shall do when I grow up.